Early Years Stories for the Foundation Stage

Following on from the success of Mal Leicester's previous books *Stories for Classroom and Assembly* and *Stories for Inclusive Schools*, this book also shows how to make use of the learning power of story – this time for young children. It provides original, themed stories and associated learning activities to promote young children's cognitive and emotional development.

The stories in this highly practical resource stimulate the child's interest and act as a springboard to the related learning games, each specifically designed to develop children's skills in the six foundation areas of learning:

- Personal, social and emotional development
- Communication, language and literacy
- Mathematical development
- Knowledge and understanding of the world
- Physical development
- Creative development.

Beautifully illustrated throughout, with extensive material that can be photocopied and used straightaway in early years environments, *Early Years Stories for the Foundation Stage* recognizes the importance of play, games, social interaction, parental involvement, multicultural education and how to enjoy learning from an early age. All early years practitioners will find this book an essential addition to their bookshelves.

Mal Leicester is Professor Emeritus at Nottingham University, based in the School of Education.

Related titles from Routledge

Stories for Circle Time and Assembly
Developing literacy skills and classroom values
Mal Leicester

Stories for Classroom and Assembly
Active learning in values education at Key Stages 1 and 2
Mal Leicester

Stories for Inclusive Schools
Developing young pupils' skills
Mal Leicester and Gill Johnson

Early Years Stories for the Foundation Stage

Ideas and inspiration for active learning

Mal Leicester

Routledge
Taylor & Francis Group

LONDON AND NEW YORK

First published 2006 by Routledge
2 Park Square, Milton Park, Abingdon, Oxon OX14 4RN

Simultaneously published in the USA and Canada
by Routledge
270 Madison Ave, New York, NY 10016

Routledge is an imprint of the Taylor & Francis Group, an informa business

© 2006 Mal Leicester

Typeset in Times New Roman by
GreenGate Publishing Services, Tonbridge, Kent
Printed and bound in Great Britain by
TJ International Ltd, Padstow, Cornwall

British Library Cataloguing in Publication Data
A catalogue record for this book is available from the British Library

Library of Congress Cataloging-in-Publication Data
Leicester, Mal.
Early years stories for the foundation stage: ideas and inspiration for
active learning / Mal Leicester.
      p. cm.
    ISBN 0-415-37603-3 (pbk. : alk. paper)
       1. Education, Preschool. 2. Storytelling. 3. Values—Study and
teaching (Elementary)—Activity programs. I. Title.

LB1140.2.L368 2006
372.67'7—dc22

                                 2006005644

ISBN10: 0–415–37603–3 (pbk)
ISBN10: 0–203–96795–X (ebk)

ISBN13: 978–0–415–37603–7 (pbk)
ISBN13: 978–0–203–96795–9 (ebk)

Contents

Acknowledgements

I am grateful to Denise Taylor and Roger Twelvetrees for helpful suggestions and to Karen Langley for assistance in preparing the manuscript.

Introduction

Stories, Activities and Learning in the Early Years

The power of **story** was used in my recently published collections for **primary school** children (*Stories for Classroom and Assembly*; *Stories for Inclusive Schools*; *Stories for Circle Time and Assembly*). This book also makes use of original, themed stories, but to promote learning in the **early years**; as with the three primary books, the stories are age-appropriate, but for pre-school children. Use of the stories provides an engaging approach and a flexible format as a way into the six foundation areas of early years learning. Activities flowing from the stories address the early learning goals of all six learning domains:

- Personal, social, emotional development
- Communication, language and literacy
- Mathematical development
- Knowledge and understanding of the world
- Physical development
- Creative development.

The book is intended for "rising-fives" teachers in schools, early years students, early years professionals and nursery school staff in both the statutory and private sectors. It is a useful resource, providing a good foundation for the children's ongoing education and development. In addition to early years staff and students, child-minders and parents will also find the stories and learning games extremely useful.

The nature of story

Story-telling has always been a powerful and basic human activity. Even before the printed word was available, people *told* stories to the next generation, passing on accumulated wisdom and helping children to make sense of their experience. In a memorable and enjoyable way, children have thus learned about themselves, about other people and about the world. Good stories both educate and entertain. In short, very young children find good stories enthralling, as they reflect their own experiences whilst expanding their horizons.

STORY IN EDUCATION

Children feel the power of story. They readily engage with stories of all kinds. Think back to your own childhood. Certainly I can vividly remember, from my own early childhood, my grandmother's stories about "the olden days", that almost unimaginable time when my parents were children and I wasn't yet born! Most of us remember our favourite childhood books with lifelong affection. It makes sense to use this love of story in education. This includes both helping children to make up stories **and** reading or telling child-friendly stories created by other people.

Listening to, telling, making-up and talking about stories can achieve many important learning goals. For example, stories can:

- Stimulate children's language development and self-confidence in discussion
- Encourage exploration of issues of interest to children
- Develop children's empathy and understanding of other people and other people's point of view
- Teach about the world in which we live
- Encourage co-operative activities
- Help to develop positive values, attitudes and qualities (e.g. fairness, tolerance of difference, kindness and wonder at the beauty and existence of the natural world)
- Perhaps above all, provide the opportunity for children to explore, in a secure environment, difficult emotions (e.g. jealousy of a new baby brother or sister) and worrying experiences (e.g. going into hospital).

Story in the early years

Short, interactive, age-appropriate stories are particularly important for very young children. We know that children from two to five benefit from structured early years learning and peer interaction. A structured but enjoyable learning, focused around stories, will help to prepare the children for "proper" school.

Of course the years up to five cover a period of rapid child development; during this period children move from simple picture books which merely label the object in the picture to books with **proper** short stories. Each of the stories in this collection is provided in both a basic and a more advanced version. The basic version gives the story at its most simple. The advanced version is more complex and detailed. You can choose one or the other, **or** you can adapt either one and tell an intermediate version to suit (but stimulate) your particular group of children. On the whole, the basic version will be told to two- and three-year-olds and the advanced to four-year-olds and rising-fives.

Similarly, the associated learning games and activities in each domain include a range – starting with the most simple.

It is in the early years that we lay down the foundations for later learning and that attitudes to learning itself are developed. Children need to learn that learning is fun (and stories provide an enjoyable form of learning) and to learn how to learn. Children who develop their love of stories are the children who will develop a love of reading – perhaps the single most powerful educational advantage they can be given.

Truth and fiction: two kinds of story

BIOGRAPHY

Children can be encouraged to tell their own stories (What did you do on your birthday?). They will also be interested to hear about things that have happened to you!

MAKE-BELIEVE

Children love make-believe stories – adventures, animal stories, stories about a child with whom they can identify, "scary" stories, realistic stories and fantasy. You can stimulate their imagination by encouraging them to make up a story in some way similar to the one you told.

BIOGRAPHY AND MAKE-BELIEVE

Children seem to know instinctively that "what actually happened" and "make-believe" (truth and fiction) are not always easy to tell apart. Autobiographical stories from "real" life are partly coloured by our imagination and memory, and "good fiction" is based on underlying truths about human nature and the human condition. Made-up stories have to be believable, so that we "accept" them while we listen or read.

Choosing the right story

You may be looking for a story with a particular theme (e.g. litter) or value (e.g. sharing). However, there are two further tests for any story which you select.

1   Is the story child-friendly?
     Is the story at an appropriate age-level? Is it accessible for very young children? Does it contain material (issues, themes, details) that will interest a young child and reflect their experiences?
2   Is the story well told?
     Is this a good story in "literary" terms? For example, does it have structure (a definite beginning, middle and end). Does it use words that children understand and use them vividly? Does it have a good pace – strong narrative drive to retain their interest? Are the characters engaging and believable?

What and when

You can use pictures, storybooks or films to tell a story. We now also have the resources of the Internet and other multi-media such as CD-Roms. You should tell or read **interactive** stories in which children repeat words or answer questions. You can return to old favourites on a regular basis. Don't forget to use your own imagination to make up stories that work for your particular children. (Perhaps a story that reflects something that happened in your playschool that week.) This particular collection of stories incorporates a comprehensive range of significant pre-school experiences, touches on pre-school issues and explores the young child's developing values and emotions.

Many teachers bring children into a circle for storytime. Stories also make a good beginning and a good end to frame the pre-school day.

Care and cognition

Although for convenience educators talk about cognition and emotion as separate aspects of the self, in practice our skills, understandings and emotions develop simultaneously as we interact with each other and with the world. This is especially true for early education. The young child learns to move from an egocentric world to one in which other people also have needs and feelings. Providing **shared** activities/play stimulates self-confidence and the beginnings of empathy for others – a so-called "theory of mind". The stories here embody an ethic of care and the associated play will be designed to promote physical and cognitive skills.

The six areas of early learning

Pre-school preparation for school is most fully achieved if the early learning goals of the six foundation areas have been addressed (see page vii). Stories and associated learning games can be focused round the learning goals. To do this:

- The teacher introduces the story and theme
- The teacher reads the story, guiding the children into the interactive element
- The teacher and children talk about the story
- The teacher guides the children into the (six) associated learning games and activities.

For example, suppose the story is about a little boy who is a bit unkind to his cat (poking her awake: see story one). He loses her and is sad. He is happy when he finds her in an unexpected place. The theme of this story is caring for our pets; the values are kindness and care.

- To introduce the session, the teacher asks the children about their pets. What are they? (Dog, cat, rabbit, etc.) What are their names? She can ask the children who do not have a pet what they would like to have if they could. She talks about how we look after our pets and about being gentle, etc.
- The teacher tells the story.
- The teacher and the children talk about the story.
- The teacher guides the children into associated learning given for the six foundation areas.

A widening circle of relationships

It is not surprising that we often sit children in a circle to listen to a story. There is something democratic and safe about sitting in a circle. Circles have no top or bottom and they contain rather than exclude. By combining the power of story and the power of the circle we open the way for a genuine sharing of the story experience and the associated discussion, emotions and learning activities.

I suggest that we can think of the child's world itself as a widening circle of relationships. With the child at the core, the circle widens out to include "the other", "the world", and the realm of "values".

For each session we will indicate the relevant pre-school themes, experiences, values, emotions and relationships.

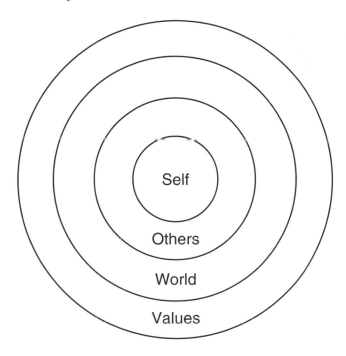

How to use this book

Each of the eight stories is the focus for one chapter. Each chapter includes discussion and learning activities for each of the six learning domains – making six learning units per chapter. These units can be used to suit your own daily/weekly structure and pace. Some of you may cover one unit per day. Others will use each of the six units on, say, each Wednesday over six weeks. You should do what best suits you and your children – including, as was previously mentioned, choice of the basic or the more advanced version of each story.

Teacher's notes introduce the theme of each chapter and link it with common early years projects. Having introduced the story you can read or tell it, showing the children the pictures and encouraging participation where appropriate. The children could sit in a circle for the story and for talking about the story. Circle time games, questions and "talk" are also provided for the "personal and social" learning domain. Deal with "difficult" vocabulary in your usual way. This is often to explain some words before you read the story and again as you come to them in your reading. A picture to colour prior to the story could also be an opportunity to introduce some of the vocabulary. You can select or add to the suggested activities. In general the youngest pre-school children will engage with the simplest activities in each unit and the older children can encompass them all should you wish. (Keep old Christmas and birthday cards. The pictures on these will be useful for some of the activities.) Should you wish to revisit and reinforce any of our stories' themes, relevant stories, songs and poems are suggested, and others you will choose for yourself. The stories feature children from various ethnic groups and reflect respect for diversity. They will be part of your values education, encouraging young children to develop positive attitudes to themselves and others.

Precious time

We hope to save you time by providing well-structured learning material, to be used with flexibility. However, in whatever way it is used the intention has been to provide enjoyable stories and games which genuinely promote those worthwhile skills and values upon which a balanced education will be built.

Professor Mal Leicester
School of Education
The University of Nottingham

Chapter 1

Was She There?

Teacher's Notes

Theme One: **Caring for Animals and Plants (including our pets).** Young children need to understand that their pets can feel pain and be hurt, just as they can themselves. We can learn how to look after them.

Associated Values: **Kindness; Respect.** Respect for living creatures should include a disposition to be kind in our treatment of animals combined with a sensible appreciation that an animal, wrongly approached, can be dangerous.

Associated Emotions: **Affection.** Young children can readily come to feel fond of their pets and can be encouraged to develop a kind, helpful, caring disposition in relation to dependent and vulnerable creatures (including younger/smaller children).

Associated Relationships: The theme and story are rich in relationships: with the **self** (being a kind person); with another **creature** (such as a family pet); with a **caring adult** (Danny's mum); with the **environment** (of our home).

Early Years Teaching

Early Years Experiences: This theme of caring for animals and plants readily taps into early years experiences of **pets and other creatures** – their food, houses, appearances, behaviour. This particular story also explores the common experience of **losing something we value**.

Early Years Topics:	This first chapter contains relevant material for teachers exploring the following topics: **Ourselves** (My Pet; My Home; My Family); **The Environment** (Our Homes); **Plants and Animals**: (Our Pets; Other Animals; Animal Noises; Plants and the Countryside).
Early Years Skills:	**The Six Learning Domains.** Pages 10–14 provide learning games and activities for each of the early years foundation areas. These are all linked to the story and its associated theme.

Session Plan: Caring for animals and plants

This timescale is provisional only. Feel free to "go with" the children's own pace. Above all, adapt the material to suit your particular group of children. There is a big difference in teaching a group of three-year-old children and a group of five-year-olds, or a mixed age group, and between teaching one or two children or a bigger group.

1   **Introduce the story**   *2–5 minutes*
     Introduce the theme   *3–5 minutes*

2   **The story**   *5–10 minutes*
     The teacher shows the illustration and suggested objects before reading the story. The story can be retold in several sessions, to be followed by a different learning activity each time. Children enjoy listening to a familiar story and may absorb new aspects each time.

3   **Talking about the story; associated stories and rhymes**   *5–10 minutes*
     The teacher uses some of the questions and discussion points given, stimulating the children to talk about the story/theme. Additionally, there are further story, poem and song suggestions provided, and a relevant traditional poem or nursery rhyme.

4   **Learning games and activities**   *5–30 minutes*
     For each story, learning activities in each of the **six** learning domains are provided. There is also a "co-operative poster" to be made and/or enjoyed.

Total time   *20–60 minutes*

1 INTRODUCE THE STORY AND THEME

To introduce the story

- The teacher tells the children that the story is about Danny and his new pet cat.
- The cat is called Marbles because she has bright green eyes. The teacher shows the children some glass marbles.
- The teacher shows the children the illustrations for the story.

To introduce the theme

- The teacher asks the children about their pets. What are they (dog, cat, rabbit, etc.)? What are their names? Ask the children who do not have a pet what they would like to have, if they could.
- Talk about how we treat our pets, for example, by being kind and gentle, not mean or rough.
- Talk about how we look after different pets. What do dogs eat? What about cats? How do we care for plants?

Additional points

- As you tell the story, once again show the two illustrations provided.
- Shake your head to indicate that the children can shout "No" to the various hiding places.
- Read it again now that the words are familiar and to allow the children to join in with each "No".

THE BASIC STORY:

Was She There?

"Here is a new pet," said Daddy.

It was a black cat. Her name was Marbles.

Marbles fell fast asleep. Danny poked her.

"Boo," he shouted.

Marbles was frightened. She ran away. Danny couldn't find her. He was sad.

At tea-time Mummy and Danny heard a noise from inside the piano. It was Marbles. Mummy lifted her out.

Danny gave Marbles some milk. He stroked her. He was happy to have her back again.

Was She There?

Was She There?

When Danny was five his daddy brought home a small black cat. She had a red collar and a white tip to her tail.

"Did she dip it in paint?" Danny said.

Mummy laughed and shook her head.

"What will you call her?" she asked.

Danny looked at his cat. Her round eyes shone like green marbles.

"Marbles," he said.

Marbles curled up and went to sleep. Danny wanted her to wake up. He poked her.

"Boo, Marbles," he shouted.

Marbles hissed at Danny and ran from the room as fast as she could.

Danny and Mummy searched the whole house to find her.

Was she under the table?

No.

Was she under the beds?

No.

Was she in the cupboard?

No.

Was she in the toy box?

No.

Was she behind the chairs?

No.

She was nowhere to be seen.

"You made her jump, Danny. It frightened her. She must have run away," Mummy said.

Danny was sad all day long. Mummy gave him a big hug. And then, they heard a thud from inside the piano. Danny and Mummy looked at each other in surprise.

Mummy reached her arm down the gap in the back of the piano. Her fingers felt something soft as fluff and she lifted it out. It was Marbles.

Mummy gave Marbles a saucer of milk. Danny watched her lap it all up with her tiny pink tongue. After that, Danny stroked her very gently.

"I'm sorry I frightened you, Marbles," he whispered. "I won't ever boo you again."

Danny stroked and stroked Marbles and she began to purr. It was a happy sound which Danny liked. He was very happy too. He and Marbles had made friends.

3 TALKING ABOUT THE STORY

The teacher and children talk about the story:

- How old was Danny?
- What did Danny's cat look like?
- Who has a pet? What colour is your dog, cat, rabbit, etc.?
- Has your pet ever been lost? Was it found?
- Have you ever lost anything else? What was it? How did you feel? Was it found?
- How did Danny frighten Marbles?
- How was he kind to her later?
- What is mean to do to your pet?
- What is kind to do to your pet?

Note: With older pre-school children you could begin to talk about why we should be kind to pets/animals.

Associated Stories, Songs, Poems and Nursery Rhymes

Stories

Cat's New House by M. Green (in *Play School Stories,* edited by Cynthia Felgate) (BBC, 1967)
The Magpie's Nest by M. Rosen (in *Play School Stories,* as above)
The Garden (in *Animal Story Book,* by Anita Hewett) (Young Puffin, 1974)
The Very Hungry Caterpillar by Eric Carle (Hamish Hamilton)
Tim Catchamouse by Sheila McCullagh (from the Puddle Lane series) (Ladybird Books)

Poems and nursery rhymes

The Three Little Kittens
Three Blind Mice
Little Bo Peep
Robin (in *A Very First Poetry Book,* edited by John Foster) (OUP)
The Farmer's In His Den (in *The Funny Family: Songs Rhymes and Games for Children,* edited by Alison McMorland) (Ward Lock Educational, 1978)
House (in *A Very First Poetry Book,* edited by John Foster) (OUP, 1979)
Ba Ba Black Sheep (in *The Young Puffin Book of Verse,* edited by Barbara Ireson) (Puffin Books)

The Three Little Kittens

The three little kittens,
They lost their mittens,
And they began to cry,
"Oh, mother dear, we sadly fear,
Our mittens we have lost."
"What! Lost your mittens,
You naughty kittens,
You shall have no pie."
Meow, meow, meow

The three little kittens,
They found their mittens,
And they began to cry,
"Oh, mother dear, see here, see here,
Our mittens we have found."
"Found your mittens!
You good little kittens,
Now you may have some pie."
Meow, meow, meow.

(This time it is not the kittens who get lost.)

Songs

Magic Penny (in *Alleluya*) (A & C Black)
The Farmer's In His Den (in *The Funny Family: Songs, Rhymes and Games for Children*, edited by Alison McMorland) (Ward Lock Educational 1978)
Old MacDonald Had a Farm (see page 12)

Note: You can find other examples of stories, songs and poems which link to the story or theme – i.e. they could be about cats, other pets, being kind/mean to animals, losing something, marbles, and, especially, showing someone being **kind**.

The Three Blind Mice

Three blind mice
See how they run
They all run after the farmer's wife
She cuts off their tails with a carving knife
Did you ever see such a thing in your life
As three blind mice.

(Wasn't the farmer's wife **mean** to the three blind mice?)

Little Bo Peep

Little Bo Peep has lost her sheep
And doesn't know where to find them,
Leave them alone,
And they will come home,
Wagging their tails behind them.

(Like Danny, Bo Peep loses her creatures.)

4 LEARNING GAMES AND ACTIVITIES

Domain 1: Personal, social and emotional development

1 Circle Time game/question
Go round the circle. Each child takes a turn to make an animal noise and the other children guess which animal it is.

2 Circle Time talk
Talk with the children about how we can look after our pets.

3 Caring for plants and animals
You will need a photocopy of page 11 and colouring crayons.
  The children colour the pictures and words. This is also good for co-ordination practice. Some children, with your help, could write their name at the bottom of the page.

4 Caring in practice
Encourage the children to do something practical. For example, they could water plants in the school garden, or take turns to water the indoor plants.

5 Role play
The children could form into pairs. Each pair chooses to be either Danny or Marbles. They role-play Danny looking after Marbles (feeding her, stroking her). After five minutes they reverse roles.

Dog	Meat
Cat	Milk
Plant	Water

Domain 2: Communication, language and literacy

1   **Noises**

Ask the children: What noise does a dog make? ("Woof, woof.") We call that barking. What noise does a cat make? ("Meow, meow.") We call that mewing.

The noise and words of various animals can be introduced: pig (snorting noise – grunting); duck (quack quack – quacking); bird (a whistling sound – whistling; singing; chirping); cow (moo moo – mooing).

2   **What do people do?**

- We talk.
- We whisper. (The children whisper this.)
- We shout. (The children shout this.)
- We whistle. (The children try to whistle.)
- We sing. (*Old MacDonald Had a Farm.*)

Old MacDonald had a farm
Ee ay, ee ay, o
And on that farm he had a cow
Ee ay, ee ay, o
With a moo moo here, and a moo moo there
Here a moo, there a moo, everywhere a moo moo
Old MacDonald had a farm
Ee ay, ee ay, o.

Domain 3: Mathematical development

Teach the children the *Five Little Ducks* song. The children sing the song. The children copy the teacher who folds down one finger for each duck, and holds up all five fingers at the end.

Five little ducks went out one day
Over the hills and far away
Mother duck said quack quack quack quack
But only four little ducks came back.
Four little ducks went out one day
Over the hills and far away
Mother duck said quack quack quack quack
But only three little ducks came back.
Three little ducks went out one day
Over the hills and far away
Mother duck said quack quack quack quack
But only two little ducks came back.
Two little ducks went out one day
Over the hills and far away
Mother duck said quack quack quack quack
But only one little duck came back.
One little duck went out one day
Over the hills and far away
Mother duck said quack quack quack quack

But no little ducks came back.
Mother duck went out one day
Over the hills and far way
Mother duck said quack quack quack quack
And all those little ducks came back.

Domain 4 – Knowledge and understanding of the world

1 A walk
Take the children for a walk around the playground, playing fields or local park. How many living things can they see?

● Trees, plants, flowers, grass, hedges, bushes.
● Dogs, cats, birds, squirrels, rabbits.
● Possibly: a bee, a fly, butterflies, dragonflies, beetles, ants, spiders, worms.

2 A collage
The children could bring back small "treasures" from their walk: Small stones, weather cones, leaves, sticks. Place a sheet of contact paper on the wall, sticky side out. Let the children stick the treasures on the paper to make a nature collage.

3 Recall game
Have the children go round a circle and each child says. "I went on a walk and I saw ...". Each child recalls one thing they saw on their walk.

4 Living and non-living things (advanced)
The children begin to categorise things as living and non-living. For example, have pictures of the following items for them to sort: a dog, a cat, a plant, a fish, a tree, a butterfly, a bird, a doll, a car, a plate with a picture of a butterfly, etc. Do not be surprised if the children mis-categorise. For example, plant as non-living and doll as living. It will take time and patience before they begin to "get" the distinction. It is complicated! However, gradually they will begin to understand that living things need food and can feel hurt (pain and sadness) and can die, and that non-living things do not need food (perhaps fuel), and do **not** feel pain or sad/happy but can be damaged or broken.

Domain 5: Physical development

Movement to music: creatures
Suggest an animal and to appropriate music the children dance as that creature. For example, they move quickly and lightly as amouse, slither as a snake, balance as a kangaroo, etc. More ambitiously, an animal dance could be created.

Domain 6: Creative development

1 Role play
The children work in pairs. One child will be the pet. What will s/he be? One child will be the owner (a grown-up). Who is s/he? What is his/her name?

The pet has to pretend to get lost. The owner has to pretend and search and find the pet. The owner strokes the pet and provides food.

The children will have to decide on the pet, where it is lost and how it is found – this role-playing stimulates their imagination and their co-operative play.

2   Tell a story

Retell the story of Marbles very briefly and very clearly.

Have the children take turns to tell the story. Have the children make up their own story about a cat (or dog).

3   Piano games

If you have access to a piano (or other instrument) take the opportunity to develop the children's listening skills and creativity with musical sounds. (For example, what does this (heavy notes) sound like? (Thunder or giants.) And this (light notes)? (Fairies.)

Co-operative poster activity

- Find a poster illustrating the song *Old MacDonald Had a Farm.* Alternatively, make your own. Best of all, have the children help you make the poster. Stick on a farmer and his dog, two cats, a field with three horses and four cows, a pond with five ducks.
- Use the poster to allow the children to take turns to identify the farmer, the dog, a cat, etc.
- Use the poster to talk about caring for these animals.
- Have the children count the number of dogs, cats, horses, etc.

Chapter 2

The Magic Unicorn

Teacher's Notes

Theme Two: **Being Brave.** Young children need to understand that we are all sometimes afraid. They can learn ways to cope with fear and have some preparation for difficult situations, such as being in hospital.

Associated Values: **Bravery: Self-Confidence; Kindness.** It is not wrong to be frightened. It is not wrong to tell someone that we are frightened. To cope with fear, including telling someone about it, is brave. It is good to be kind and helpful to someone who is afraid.

Associated Emotions: **Fear; Loving Concern.** We cannot be brave without fear. We want children to develop a protective, loving concern for those in fear and to be open and unashamed of their own fears.

Associated Relationships: The theme and story are rich in relationships: with the **self** (feeling fear and being a brave person); with **another creature** (the Magic Unicorn); with a **caring adult** (Nurse Flora); with the **environment** (the hospital); with the **natural world** (seaside and flowers).

Early Years Teaching

Early Years Experiences: This theme of "being brave" readily taps into early years experiences of **frightening situations** such as going to hospital, having an injection, going to the dentist, going away from home for the first time without Mum, being bullied, being shouted at, etc. Children also have **favourite toys** and books and objects and people, and the world is a wonderful, magical place.

Early Years Topics: This second chapter contains relevant material for teachers exploring the following topics: **Ourselves** (Our Feelings); **Toys** (Puzzles; Jigsaws); **People Who Help Us** (Doctors and Nurses); **Materials** (Wood. What is it used for? Where does it come from? How does it feel, etc.?)

Early years Skills: **The Six Learning Domains.** Pages 23–6 provide learning games and activities for each of the early years foundation areas. These are all linked to the story and its associated theme.

Session Plan: Feelings – fear and being brave

This timescale is provisional only. Feel free to "go with" the children's own pace. Above all, adapt the material to suit your particular group of children. There is a big difference in teaching a group of three-year-old children and a group of five-year-olds, or a mixed age group, and between teaching one or two children or a bigger group.

1   **Introduce the story**   *2–5 minutes*
    Introduce the theme   *3–5 minutes*

2   **The story**   *5–10 minutes*

The teacher shows the illustration and suggested objects before reading the story. The story can be retold in several sessions, to be followed by a different learning activity each time. Children enjoy listening to a familiar story and may absorb new aspects each time.

3   **Talking about the story; associated stories and rhymes**   *5–10 minutes*

The teacher uses some of the questions and discussion points given, stimulating the children to talk about the story/theme. Additionally, there are further story, poem and song suggestions provided, and a relevant traditional poem or nursery rhyme.

4   **Learning games and activities**   *5–30 minutes*

For each story, learning activities in each of the **six** learning domains are provided. There is also a "co-operative poster" to be made and/or enjoyed.

| **Total time** | *20–60 minutes* |

1 INTRODUCE THE STORY AND THEME

To introduce the story

- The teacher tells the children that the story is about Flora who goes to hospital for an operation.
- Flora is afraid but a picture of a unicorn helps her to be brave. The teacher shows the children pictures of "magic" creatures – fairies, mermaids, unicorns.
- The teacher tells the children that Flora's operation was to make her better.

To introduce the theme

- The teacher asks the children if they have ever been to hospital? How did they feel? What nice things happened?
- How many children have had an injection? How did they feel? Why is it good to have injections?
- What or who has helped them when they were afraid? How?
- How can you help someone else who is frightened?

Additional points

- Try not to introduce apprehension/fear about hospital. A young child may not yet have this!
- Try to enable the children to understand that we all sometimes feel afraid and that there are people and things that can help us to "be brave" – including our own imagination/thoughts.
- Try to ensure that children who may have to go to hospital after this story will be better prepared for the experience. For example, explain that doctors and nurses are there to help us. The hospital is there to make us better when we are ill. We can take toys and books. Our mummy and daddy and friends can visit us in the hospital.

2 THE BASIC STORY:

The Magic Unicorn

Flora was gong into hospital to have an operation. Mummy went with her. At the hospital, they did a jigsaw. The picture was a beautiful unicorn.

"See his golden horn," said Mummy. "He's magic."

Flora liked the unicorn.

In the operation room a kind nurse held Flora's hand.

"You'll go to sleep, sweetheart," she said, "and when you wake up you'll be better."

Flora dreamed she was at the seaside, riding on her white unicorn. When she woke up, Mummy was there.

"You're better," she said. "And you were brave."

Daddy came and gave her a book of magic creatures. It had a picture of Flora's unicorn. When Flora went home, she took her book with her. Whenever Flora felt poorly or frightened, she looked at her unicorn and felt a bit better.

2 THE ADVANCED STORY:

The Magic Unicorn

The Magic Unicorn

Mum drove Flora to the hospital. Flora was having her tonsils taken out, to make her sore throat better.

"You can play in the playroom while you wait," said Nurse Rose.

Flora liked it in the playroom. She found a wooden jigsaw. It showed a white horse galloping on a yellow beach.

"That's a unicorn," said Mum. "See his golden horn."

Flora undid the jigsaw pieces and began to put them together again. She enjoyed bringing the lovely unicorn back, piece by piece.

"What a lovely picture," said the Nurse. "See the pretty flowers round his neck. Your name means "flower", Flora, and I have a flower name too."

The next day, when it was time for Flora's operation, Nurse Rose said, "Don't worry, Flora, I'll stay with you. You'll have a sleep and when you wake up your throat will soon be better, and Mum will still be here."

Nurse Rose held Flora's hand while the doctor did an injection. Flora was brave about it. She thought about the unicorn. She imagined him with flowers in his mane. When she fell asleep, she dreamed that she was riding him over the long yellow sand.

When Flora woke up she was in a different ward but Mum was still there, smiling down at her. Later Dad came. He gave her a book of magic creatures. It had pictures of fairies and mermaids, and best of all, at the very end, a picture of a white unicorn. He was looking out of the page, straight at Flora. It was her unicorn! She could see his golden horn and his swishy tail, and there were the red flowers in his flowing white hair.

The next day Flora was happy to go home. She took her book of magic creatures with her and after that, whenever she was afraid, she looked at her magic unicorn and he helped her to feel brave.

3 TALKING ABOUT THE STORY

The teacher and children talk about the story:

- What does Flora find in the hospital playroom?
- In the jigsaw picture, where was the unicorn? (On the beach. On the sand. At the seaside. On an island.)
- What does "Flora" mean?
- Who in the class has a name with a meaning? You could use a "baby" name book to tell the children the meaning of their names.
- What helped Flora to be brave?
- What was Flora's book about?
- What creatures do the children like? (Seahorses. Goldfish. Butterflies. Peacocks.)

Note: With older pre-school children you could begin to talk about real and pretend creatures (seahorses, peacocks, butterflies; unicorns, mermaids, fairies).

Associated stories, songs, poems and nursery rhymes

Stories

Myths, legends, fairy-tales about fabulous creatures such as dragons, fairies, mermaids, unicorns.

Postman Pat series by John Cunliffe (Handy Hippo Books from Scholastic)
Can't You Sleep, Little Bear? by Martin Waddell (Walker Books)
The Owl who was Afraid of the Dark by Jill Tomlinson (Young Puffin)
The Very Busy Spider by Eric Carle (Hamish Hamilton)
Where the Wild Things Are Maurice Sendak (Bodley Head)
One Spinning Spider by Sally Crabtree (Gullane Children's Books)

Songs

Miss Molly had a Dolly who was Sick, Sick, Sick
Sing a Song of People (in *Tinder-box: Assembly Book*, by Sue Nicholls) (A&C Black)

Poems and nursery rhymes

Little Miss Muffet
Incy Wincy Spider

Little Miss Muffet

Little Miss Muffet sat on her tuffet,
Eating her curds and whey.
Along came a spider and sat down beside her,
And frightened Miss Muffet away.

The Milkmen (in *The Young Puffin Book of Verse*, edited by Barbara Ireson) (Puffin Books)
The Dustbin Men (in *A Very First Poetry Book*, edited by John Foster) (OUP)

Incy Wincy Spider

Incy Wincy Spider climbed up the water spout,
Down came the rain and washed the spider out.
Out came the sun and dried up all the rain,
So Incy Wincy Spider climbed up the spout again.

Note: You can find other examples of stories, songs and poems which link to the story or theme – i.e. they could be about magical creatures, hospital, being poorly, being frightened, names, helping, people who help us, nurses.

4   LEARNING GAMES AND ACTIVITIES

Domain 1: Personal, social and emotional development

1   Circle Time game/question

Go round the circle asking the children to name one thing they are afraid of. (The dark. Spiders. Snakes. Angry dogs or cats. Bullies, etc.)

2   Circle Time talk

Discuss what we can do to feel better about these particular fears. Discuss what helps *you* to be brave.

Domain 2: Communication, language and literacy

1   Little Miss Muffet

Teach the nursery rhyme to the children. After this, in pairs, the children can pretend to be a spider and Miss Muffet and act out the rhyme as you repeat it. (Do this twice so that the children can reverse roles.) Miss Muffet pretends to eat and the spider sits and makes a scary noise or perhaps says "boo." Miss Muffet runs away.

2   What things are we afraid of?

Who is afraid of spiders? Or snakes? What else? (The dark. Injections. Bullies.)

Have a box with a lid, and place a toy snake inside. Tell the children that nothing in the box could hurt them, but pretend it is a real snake. Volunteers take turns to put their hand into the box. How do they feel?

Domain 3: Mathematical development

1   How many? Photocopy the unicorn on page 24 and give a copy to each child. Ask the children:

- How many horns does the unicorn have? The unicorn has one horn. (They point to the horn.)
- How many tails does the unicorn have? The unicorn has one tail. (They point to the tail.)
- How many ears does the unicorn have? The unicorn has two ears. (They point to the ears.)
- How many flowers are in the unicorn's picture? The unicorn has three flowers in his picture. (They point to the flowers.)
- How many legs does the unicorn have? The unicorn has four legs. (They point to the legs.)

This can be repeated with other animal pictures.

2   Jigsaw picture

Help the children to stick their unicorn picture onto card. They cut the picture into four pieces to make a jigsaw. They make up this picture again – or swap and try to "do" another child's jigsaw.

3   Add flowers

The children draw three flowers in the unicorn's mane.

Domain 4: Knowledge and understanding of the world

People who help us

This is an ideal opportunity to focus on this popular early years project. Here are some ideas:

- **Clothing, equipment, toy cars**

  Collect a range of representative clothes (e.g. toy nurse in uniform, fireman's helmet, policeman's helmet) and equipment (doctor's stethoscope, milk bottle, blackboard) and toy cars (fire engine, ambulance, police car, dust cart, tractor, milk cart).

  Have the children identify "who helps us" associated with each. (Nurse in uniform – nurses. Ambulance – ambulance driver, etc.)

- **Visiting speakers**

  Invite visiting speakers to come and talk to the children about what they do. (Community nurse. Health visitor. Community policeman. Volunteer in a charity shop, etc.)

- **Emergency services**

  Children love using phones and toy phones. They can practise dialling 999. When do we do this? **Only** when ... What would we say? Which service? Your address?

Domain 5: Physical development

1 **Healthy exercise**

   Do gentle exercises with the children to exercise different parts of their bodies.

2 **Healthy eating**

   This is a good opportunity to focus on the topic of healthy eating.

A balanced diet must consist of the following.

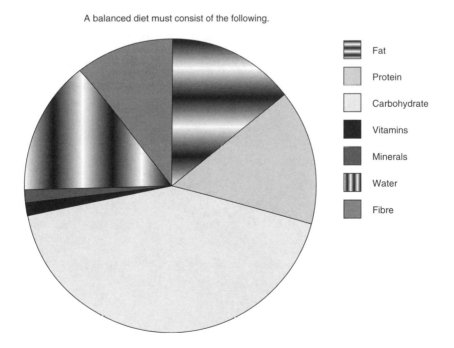

Fat

Protein

Carbohydrate

Vitamins

Minerals

Water

Fibre

Domain 6: Creative development

1   Classroom people who help us

Have the children create a "People Who Help Us" picture for the classroom wall. If you have a stack of magazines the children could cut out appropriate people and vehicles, etc., or bring these from home. These are stuck, overlapping, to form a collage. Alternatively each child could draw a person who helps us, and these could be stuck all along a sheet.

2   Tell a dream

The children could tell about a dream they had that was frightening. By saying, "What could have happened next? What could you have done?" help the children to shape the dream into a story, with a beginning, middle and **reassuring** end.

Co-operative poster activities

1   Find a poster illustrating Little Miss Muffet. Use the poster to allow the children to take turns to identify Miss Muffet, the spider, the curds and whey, etc. and to point to colours and shapes in the poster.

> Talk with the children about what else might frighten Miss Muffet.
> Suppose the spider is a kind spider. What might he have said instead of "Boo?"
> Have the children recite the nursery rhyme.

2   Let the children draw and/or cut out a variety of animals to make their own animal ABC poster, e.g.: A is for Ape. B is for Bear. C is for Cat. D is for Duck. E is for Elephant. F is for Frog. G is for Gull (or Giraffe). H is for Hare (or Hedgehog). I is for Insect. J is for Jellyfish. K is for Kangaroo. L is for Lion. M is for Monkey. N is for Newt. O is for Octopus (or Ostrich). P is for Penguin. Q is for Queen Bee. R is for Robin. S is for Snake. T is for Tiger. U is for Unicorn (of course). V is for Vulture. W is for Whale (or Wasp). X is for X-ray fish. Z is for Zebra.

Of course you could have different choices. Divide the sheet into 30 spaces and use four for the title "Animal ABC" to leave 26 (see page 27). Once the children have stuck their picture (or drawing) into the correct square on the chart, it can be used for identifying the creature (point to the elephant) and for recognising letters, e.g. S (snake) and simpler words, e.g. Cat.

Animal A B C	A	B	C
	D	E	F
G	H	I	J	K
L	M	N	O	P
Q	R	S	T	U
V	W	X	Y	Z

Chapter 3

Someone to Play With

Teacher's Notes

Theme Three: **Anger.** Young children feel overwhelmed by their sudden anger (tantrums), which are often a response to frustration. They can learn to cope with these episodes and, more gradually, to control them. A secondary theme of this story is that we all like to enjoy time with a friend. (Chapter 6 takes the theme of friendship directly.)

Associated Values: **Understanding and Coping with Our Emotions.** It is not wrong to feel angry. We all feel angry sometimes. It is good to learn to control our anger and express it in positive ways.

Associated Emotions: Emotions often associated with the emotion of anger include **frustration** and **disappointment**; good self-esteem helps us to control our anger. For a young child the world can be a very frustrating place. (They often feel powerless.) They need to protest. Assertiveness is positive provided it is not out of our control. Anger is a complex emotion arising from good reasons (e.g. response to injustice) and poor reasons (damaged ego; impatience). We can learn to be sorry about our anger where appropriate, and understanding about the anger of another.

Associated Relationships: The theme and story are rich in relationships: with the **self** (our feelings of anger); with **others** (a new friend; a caring adult); with the **environment** (the garden).

Early Years Teaching

Early Years Experiences: This theme of "Anger" readily taps into early years experiences of **disappointment** and **tantrums**. In this story we also tap into the child's wish for, and pleasure in having, a **friend to play with** and (without someone to play with) their occasional **boredom**.

Early Years Topics: This third chapter contains relevant material for teachers exploring the following topics: **Ourselves** (Our Emotions); **Toys** (that we can play with by ourselves, that we play with with others); **The Environment** (Gardens; Litter; Things we Find in the Garden; Gardening); **Making Friends** (New Friends; Making Up; Being a Good Friend).

Early Years Skills: **The Six Learning Domains.** Pages 38–42 provide learning games and activities for each of the early years foundation areas. These are all linked to the story and its associated theme.

Session Plan: Dealing with anger

This timescale is provisional only. Feel free to "go with" the children's own pace. Above all, adapt the material to suit your particular group of children. There is a big difference in teaching a group of three-year-old children and a group of five-year-olds, or a mixed age group, and between teaching one or two children or a bigger group.

1 **Introduce the story**   *2–5 minutes*
    Introduce the theme   *3–5 minutes*

2 **The story**   *5–10 minutes*

The teacher shows the illustration and suggested objects before reading the story. The story can be retold in several sessions, to be followed by a different learning activity each time. Children enjoy listening to a familiar story and may absorb new aspects each time.

3 **Talking about the story; associated stories and rhymes**   *5–10 minutes*

The teacher uses some of the questions and discussion points given, stimulating the children to talk about the story/theme. Additionally, there are further story, poem and song suggestions provided, and a relevant traditional poem or nursery rhyme.

4 **Learning games and activities**   *5–30 minutes*

For each story, learning activities in each of the **six** learning domains are provided. There is also a "co-operative poster" to be made and/or enjoyed.

Total time | *20–60 minutes*

1 INTRODUCE THE STORY AND THEME

To introduce the story

- The teacher tells the children that the story is about Akram who wants someone to play with.
- Akram enjoys playing with Joe very much and feels a huge anger when they have to stop for lunch.
- The teacher shows the children a beautiful coloured sari and, again, some marbles. She shows the children the illustrations for the story.

To introduce the theme

- The teacher asks the children what has made them feel angry.
- She says that we are all angry sometimes. Is it a nice feeling? No.
- She talks about ways we can deal with our anger, such as writing about it, talking to a friend, or doing something active, like kicking a football about.

Additional points

- As you tell the story, show the illustration provided.
- Use the story as an opportunity to be positive about different ways of dressing.

2 THE BASIC STORY:

Someone to Play With

Akram had no one to play with.

"Shall I come and play with you?" said the new boy next door. His name was Joe.

Akram and Joe had a great time. They played catch until Akram threw the ball too high and it landed in Mr Knowles' garden.

"Time for lunch now," said Mum. "Time for Joe to go home."

Akram felt very angry.

"No, no, no," he shouted.

"Don't shout, boy," said Mr Knowles. "Here's the ball."

Akram was surprised. He stopped shouting and caught the ball.

"You can come and play with Joe tomorrow," said Joe's mum.

Akram was happy. He would play with Joe again.

Someone to Play With

Someone to Play With

Akram and Mum were in the garden. Mum was hanging out the washing. She propped up the washing line and a rainbow of saris curved in the breeze.

"I wish I had a brother," Akram grumbled. "What's the use of a garden if there's no-one to play with?"

There was a new boy next door. He gave Akram a friendly grin.

"Shall I come and play with you?" he asked.

Akram nodded shyly.

"Hi, I'm Jane Cox," the boy's mum said. "We moved in yesterday."

"Hi," said Akram's mum. "Come and have a cup of tea while the boys have a play."

They went into Akram's house, leaving the two boys in the garden.

"I'm Joe," said the new boy.

"I'm Akram."

Joe pulled a blue ball out of his pocket.

"See your mum's line of washing? You stand on that side and we'll play catch!"

Akram ran to the other side of the washing line.

"Ready," he said.

Joe threw the ball over the clothes line.

"Catch!" he shouted.

Akram caught the ball. He threw it back to Joe.

"Catch!" he shouted.

Joe caught it and threw it back.

"Catch!" he shouted. He liked shouting catch.

On Akram's sixth shout he threw the ball very high. It sailed over the wall into Mr Knowles' garden.

"Never mind, I know another game," said Joe. "We'll put litter in that empty washing basket. Your Mum will be pleased.

Each time Akram or Joe found a piece of litter they shouted "Catch" as they threw it into the basket. Even collecting litter was a great game with Joe.

After that Joe pulled five marbles out of his pocket. They sparkled in the sunlight and Akram saw swirls of different colours deep inside each one.

Akram really enjoyed the game of marbles. It was the best game of all, but before long the two mums came back into the garden.

"Time for lunch, Akram," said Akram's mum.

"Time to go now, Joe," said Joe's mum.

Akram felt a huge, hot anger swell up inside him like a tornado. It streamed out of his mouth in a scream of protest. "No! No! No!"

Suddenly a head appeared over the high wall. It was Mr Knowles from next door.

"Don't shout so loud, lad," he said. "I'm not that deaf, you know." He threw the blue ball towards Akram.

Akram was so surprised his scream stopped with a gulp. He caught the ball and gave it back to Joe.

"Bye, Akram," said Joe's mum. "Tomorrow you can come and play in our garden."

Akram was happy. He realised that playing with Joe hadn't ended. It had only just begun.

3 TALKING ABOUT THE STORY

The teacher and children talk about the story. (This could be done in a circle or as part of your Circle Time.)

- Do you know what colours are in a rainbow? Red, Orange, Yellow, Green, Blue, Indigo, Violet. Has anyone ever see a rainbow? When do we see them?
- What colour flowers have you seen in a garden?
- What games did Akram and Joe play together?
- Why did Akram feel angry?
- What made Akram stop screaming?
- Why was Akram happy in the end?

Associated stories, songs, poems and nursery rhymes

Stories

It Won't Work by Janice Amos (from the Good Friends series) (Cherrytree Books)
The Garden (in *Animal Story Book,* by Anita Hewett) (Young Puffin)
Planting a Rainbow by Lois Ehlert (Gollancz)
Peter Gets Angry by Maryann Macdonald (Dinosaur Publications)
The I was so Mad I Could Have Split Book by Gisela Frisen and Per Ekholm (A&C Black)
Cross Patch by M. Barker (in *Tell Me Another Story*) (Young Puffin)
The Temper Tantrum Book by E. M. Preston (Picture Puffin)

Songs

The Litter Bin Song (in *Songs From Play School*) (BBC. A&C Black)
The Tidy Song (in *Tinder-box* by Sylvia Barratt) (A&C Black)
In the Garden (in *Every Colour Under the Sun*) (Ward Lock Educational)
Getting Angry (in *Every Colour Under the Sun*) (Ward Lock Educational)
Tiny Creatures (in *Sing as You Grow* by Brenda Piper) (Ward Lock Educational)

Poems and nursery rhymes

The Dustbin Men (in *A Very First Poetry Book,* edited by John Foster) (OUP)
Joachim the Dustman by Kurt Baumen and David McKee (A&C Black)
Is a Caterpillar Ticklish? edited by Adrian Rumble (Young Puffin)

Good and Horrid

There was a little girl
And she had a little curl
Right in the middle of her forehead,
When she was good
She was very, very good
But when she was bad she was horrid.

Note: You can find other examples of stories, songs and poems which link to the theme (anger) or to the story (litter, gardens, playing).

4   LEARNING GAMES AND ACTIVITIES

Domain 1: Personal, social and emotional development

1   **Circle Time game/question**
"Pass the Face" … Show the children how your face can show your feelings. Make a sad face, a happy face, an angry face. Pass the sad face to the first child. That child passes it to the next child – and so on, round the circle. Pass a happy face. Pass an angry face.

2   **Circle Time talk**
Sit in a circle with the children. Go round the circle asking:

- **"What makes you angry?"** Prompt some ideas, e.g. best friend, brother, parent, teacher; unkind actions, unfair actions, breaking your toy, not being allowed to do something.
- **"What makes you angry with yourself?"** (Not being able to do something such as tie shoelaces, spoiling my picture, saying something unkind that I didn't mean to say.)
- **"How does being angry feel?"** (Cross and upset, hot and bothered, mean, frightened and miserable.
- **"How does being angry make us behave?"** (Being mean or unkind, shouting, spoiling things, breaking things, quarrelling, losing friends.)
- **"What can we do to deal with our anger?"** (Tell someone who is understanding and kind how you feel; say sorry if your anger made you do something mean; draw a picture of how angry you feel – doing the angry picture will help you feel better; punch a pillow or play at stamping round like an angry bear.)

Domain 2: Communication, language and literacy

Angry and peaceful words
Still in the circle, go round and ask the children to say whether each of these words is a angry word or a peaceful word:

| crash | roar | kind | hot | calm | quarrel |
| gentle | rainbow | quiet | slap | thunder | dream |

If the answer is not what you expect, ask why they think that. They may have a good reason (e.g. an angry dream).
   Still in the circle, ask the children for their own angry and peaceful words; sad and happy words; kind and mean words.

Domain 3: Mathematical development

1   **Safe destruction**
How many bricks can the children build into a tower before it crashes down? One, two, three, four …? When the children know how many bricks they can "do", let them demolish their own tower. "Crash!"

2   Counting on the page
Photocopy page 40 for each child.

- How many bricks are there? (Picture 1)
- How many bricks are there? (Picture 2)
- How many birds are there? (Picture 3)
- How many butterflies are there? (Picture 4)
- How many flowers are there? (Picture 5)

3   Counting outdoors
Take a walk in the garden and let the children count flowers. How many red flowers can you see? How many white flowers in this flower bed? How many birds can we count?

1

2

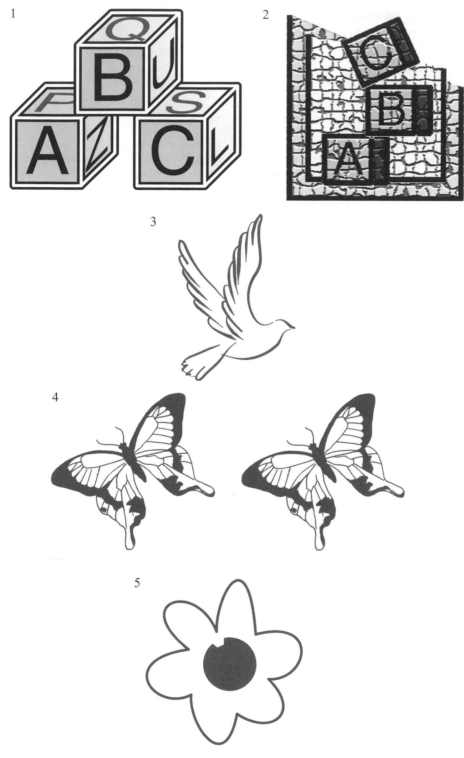

3

4

5

Domain 4: Knowledge and understanding of the world

1   **Growing a seed**
    Allow the children to plant grass or cress seeds and water them and gradually watch them grow. You could cut a large potato in half, scoop out some flesh and put damp cotton wool on top. Sprinkle with grass seeds. When the grass grows, the children can make a hedgehog by adding a nose and eyes. (Perhaps this could be timed to chime in with Chapter 5 – a story with a hedgehog.)

2   **Nature table**
    On the garden walk, encourage the children to collect leaves, stones, twigs, conkers, etc., and begin to create, or add to, a nature table.

Domain 5: Physical development

Have the children crouch, pretending to be bulbs or seeds in the ground. Gradually they "grow", getting taller and taller and stretching their arms until they are on tiptoe, fully stretched. "We are growing and growing and growing!"

Domain 6: Creative development

1   **A peaceful place**
    Gardens are peaceful places. Close your eyes. Imagine you are in a beautiful, peaceful garden. It has a wall all round it. Beautiful red leaves cover the walls. What do you see in your garden? Imagine you are walking round. See the flowers. Red ones. Blue ones. White ones. Watch a bird hopping on the grass. Now watch a beautiful butterfly. She is resting on a white flower. Now she is fluttering round the garden. There is a fountain in the garden. Watch the light sparkle on the water. Imagine you can hear the gentle sound of water. Look down and see the fish swimming round and round. Perhaps you see a frog. He is sitting on a big leaf on the water and croaking. Now someone kind comes into the garden and smiles at you. Look at who it is and see what they are wearing. What do they say? When the children open their eyes they can tell you who came into the garden and smiled. What was s/he wearing? What did s/he say?

2   **Expressing anger**
    It helps us to deal with anger if we can express it creatively – in a picture or poem. Let the children draw a picture called "Anger." Or they could write a poem. Here is one I wrote in a story about an angry boy:

Not Fair
Like a charging bull
Or like a baited bear
I'm red in my head
Because it's not fair.
I feel a roaring rage
Like a lion in a cage
I want to stamp and shout
And let my lion out.

Co-operative poster activity

Draw a garden wall round the edge of a big sheet. Each child can draw something on a small sheet and these can be stuck into the garden. They might draw a flower, a bird, a butterfly.

They can use the poster to identify colours and objects, and for counting the flowers and birds and butterflies.

Chapter 4

Fun Country Fair

Teacher's Notes

Theme Four: **Getting Lost.** Many young children have the frightening experience of getting lost. It is important that they know (safe) ways to deal with the situation.

Associated Values: **Sensible Behaviour.** "Sensible" behaviour can help prevent the child getting lost – but they need to know what this is in concrete detail. "Keep hold of Mummy's hand." "Don't go off on your own." "Don't go off with people you don't know." Also, "sensible" behaviour can help them to be safely found. (In a big shop, tell the lady at the checkout counter. Tell a policeman or lollipop lady.)

Associated Emotions: **Fear; Relief.** As was discussed in Chapter 2, we all experience fear. We need to be perceptive and understanding about each child's fears and anxieties.

Associated Relationships: With the **self** (developing a sense of responsibility); with **others** (developing a sense of whom to trust); with the **environment** (big public events/places – funfair; car boot sale; garden party; big shopping area or store, etc.).

Early Years Teaching

Early Years Experiences: Many young children have the frightening experience of **being lost.** This story provides the opportunity to talk about this experience. Your aims will be: to make children less likely to get lost; to help them think about a sensible (safe) way to get found.

Early Years Topics: This fourth chapter contains relevant material for teachers exploring the following topics: **Ourselves** (Keeping safe); **Weather/Seasons** (Rain, etc. How it makes us feel. Clothes we wear. Connection with the topic of Seasons); **Shape and Space** (Relative size. Which is bigger); **The Environment** (Leisure environments: fairs, seaside, swimming baths, shopping centres).

Early Years Skills: **The Six Learning Domains.** Pages 52–7 provide learning games and activities for each of the early years foundation areas. These are all linked to the story and its associated theme.

Session Plan: Getting lost; keeping safe

This timescale is provisional only. Feel free to "go with" the children's own pace. Above all, adapt the material to suit your particular group of children. There is a big difference in teaching a group of three-year-old children and a group of five-year-olds, or a mixed age group, and between teaching one or two children or a bigger group.

1 **Introduce the story**   *2–5 minutes*

   Introduce the theme   *3–5 minutes*

2 **The story**   *5–10 minutes*

   The teacher shows the illustration and suggested objects before reading the story. The story can be retold in several sessions, to be followed by a different learning activity each time. Children enjoy listening to a familiar story and may absorb new aspects each time.

3 **Talking about the story; associated stories and rhymes**   *5–10 minutes*

   The teacher uses some of the questions and discussion points given, stimulating the children to talk about the story/theme. Additionally, there are further story, poem and song suggestions provided, and a relevant traditional poem or nursery rhyme.

4 **Learning games and activities**   *5–30 minutes*

   For each story, learning activities in each of the **six** learning domains are provided. There is also a "co-operative poster" to be made and/or enjoyed.

Total time *20–60 minutes*

1 INTRODUCE THE STORY AND THEME

To introduce the story

- The teacher tells the children the story is about a little girl called Molly who got lost at a funfair.
- The little girl got lost because she went off on her own when her daddy wasn't looking.
- The teacher shows the children the illustration for the story.

To introduce the theme

- The teacher asks the children if they have ever been lost. What happened? How did you get found again?
- Talk about how not to get lost.
- Talk about what we can do if we are lost.

Additional points

- You can use this story and theme as part of a general project on Safety.
- You could show the children a picture/poster of a funfair. Have they ever been to a fair? Where else do we find roundabouts and slides? (Playground.)
- You could show them a "twisty" stick of barley sugar.

2 THE BASIC STORY:

Fun Country Fair

Molly went to the country fair with Daddy and her big brother Tom.

Tom went off to the big bouncy slide.

When Daddy wasn't looking, Molly also went off by herself.

She enjoyed a roundabout ride on a bright yellow horse, but it began to rain. Molly got soaking wet. There were animals at the fair. A big cow mooed at Molly. She was frightened. She wanted her daddy but she was lost. She was scared she might never find him again.

Molly saw Tom on the bouncy slide. She ran to her brother and he phoned Dad.

Dad came and found Molly and gave her a big hug.

"I was very worried," he said.

"I won't ever go off again," said Molly. "I don't like being lost!"

THE ADVANCED STORY:

Fun Country Fair

Fun Country Fair

"Look, Molly." Tom pointed at a poster with a picture of a clown. The clown was juggling red letters. "Funniston Fun Country Fair", Tom read.

"Hooray," shouted Molly. "We're here at last!"

Dad parked the car in the field.

"See you later," Tom said. "I'm off to the bouncy slide." Molly's big brother was allowed to go off by himself.

Molly could see a roundabout with brightly painted horses. She decided to go on her own – just this once, for only a minute, for one tiny ride. She ran to the roundabout and climbed on a yellow horse. She held onto a golden pole. It was twisty like a stick of barley sugar. The music started. The horses rode up and down and round and round. They galloped faster and faster. Molly clung on tight, tingling with excitement.

After the horse ride it began to rain. All the people ran for shelter. Molly ran too. She stood in a big tent looking out. The heavy rain bounced on the ground and made puddles. A sudden noise, louder than the pouring rain, made Molly jump. A loud-speaker behind her had crackled into life. Molly listened in amazement. The announcement was all about her! It said she was lost and her dad was looking for her.

Molly ran out into the rain to find Dad. The rain drenched her hair and trickled into her eyes and her coat was soon soaking wet. She ran and ran, until her legs began to ache. Suppose she never found him again? Molly slowed to a stop, feeling scared.

The rain stopped. A nearby gate opened and men began to lead out huge cows. One mooed at Molly, straining on its rope. She hid behind a caravan and began to cry. What should she do? How could she find her daddy?

In the distance, towering above everything else, Molly could see the giant blue and red slide. It was bouncy like a bouncy castle. The sun was out again and children climbed up each side and slid down the middle. Molly remembered that Tom had gone there.

"He might still be there," Molly thought.

The Story

Keeping the bouncy slide in sight, Molly ran all the way. When she reached it, she looked up and jiggled with joy. Right at the top, lowering himself onto a mat, was Tom, her big brother. Molly stood at the bottom and watched him hurtle towards her. He landed on the bouncy part at the bottom and caught sight of Molly. He gave a big grin and jumped off the slide.

"There you are!"

He took out his mobile and rang Dad.

"She's here at the slide with me," he said.

A few moments later Molly saw Dad racing towards her, as fast as the galloping horses. He swept Molly up into his arms.

"I've been so worried," he told her.

"I'm sorry, Daddy. I won't ever get lost again!" promised Molly.

Dad gave her a long, long hug.

3 TALKING ABOUT THE STORY

The teacher and children talk about the story:

- Why was Tom allowed to go off on his own?
- Why didn't Daddy see Molly go off?
- How did Molly feel while she was lost?
- Have you ever got soaking wet in the rain? Or been scared by a big animal?
- How did Daddy feel while Molly was lost?
- Have you ever been to a funfair?
- Have you been on a bouncy castle, or a big slide or a roundabout?

Associated stories, songs, poems and nursery rhymes

Stories

My Naughty Little Sister at the Fair (in *My Naughty Little Sister* by Dorothy Edwards) (Penguin Books)
Hansel and Gretel

Songs

Raindrops (in *Child Education* magazine, Infant Projects 51) (Scholastic)
Rain and Sun (in *Alleluya*!) (A&C Black)
I Love the Sun (in *Someone's Singing Lord* by Beatrice Harrop) (A&C Black)

Poems and nursery rhymes

Five Little Ducks (see p 12)
Incy Wincy Spider (see p 22)
Ride-a-Cock-Horse (see below)
Rain Songs (see below)

Ride-a-Cock-Horse

Ride-a-Cock-Horse
To Banbury Cross
To see a fine lady on a fine horse
With rings on her fingers and bells on her toes
She shall have music wherever she goes

Rain Songs

It's raining, it's pouring
The old man's snoring
He went to bed and bumped his head
And never got up in the morning

Dr Foster went to Gloucester
In a shower of rain
He stepped in a puddle

Right up to his middle
And never went there again

Rain rain go away
Come again on washing day
Don't come back 'till Christmas Day
Little Akram wants to play

(You can make up variations of this rhyme.)

4 LEARNING GAMES AND ACTIVITIES

Domain 1: Personal, social and emotional development

1   Circle Time game/question

It is useful if children learn their names and addresses as soon as possible. Ask the first child in the circle: "What is your name?" He/she says "My name is ..." and adds their full name. The child then asks the next child and so on round the circle. You can go round again with "Where do you live?" and "I live at ..." If a child doesn't know his/her address, you can supply the address for the child to repeat after you.

2   Circle Time talk

Again, use a circle to talk to the children about not getting lost and what to do if we are lost. It is difficult to teach young children to keep safe. (Very young children do not know that a stranger is anyone you don't know.) You can tell them not to go off on their own, like Molly did, and teach them their name and address. Some might learn their telephone number. A wider session on keeping safe could also include hot things and sharp things. (There is a good section on "Keeping safe" in *Circle Time for the Very Young*, by Margaret Collins, Lucky Duck Publishing.) You could also make **name cards** with each child's name on. If you do these in pencil, you could help the children to go over the lines with a coloured felt-tip pen. Use the name cards at Circle Time. They will soon recognise their own name and some of the others.

3   Visiting speaker

This is an opportunity to invite a speaker (such as a policeman or community nurse or lollipop lady) to talk about their work and some aspect of "being safe".

Domain 2: Communication, language and literacy

1   Story picture

Get the children to do a picture of Molly while she is lost and a picture of Molly being found. Encourage them to tell Molly's story as you talk about their pictures.

2   A new story

Get the children to do a picture of another child, Jack, when he is lost at the seaside. They do another picture of Jack when he is found.

The children talk about their pictures and realise that they have made up their own story. Well done!

3   Rain on me

Teach the children this rhyme.

> *Pitter, patter goes the rain*
> *Pitter, patter once again*
> *Pitter, patter at the fair*
> *Pitter patter on my hair*
>
> *Rain on the green grass*
> *Rain on the tree*
> *Rain on the housetops*
> *But not on me*

In the first verse they use their fingers to show raindrops – out there and then on their head. In the second they pretend to put up an umbrella and hold it over their head. Alternatively they step into a (pretend) shelter and on "not on me" they shake their head.

Later they can suggest other "outside" words to replace the traditional "green grass".

Rain on the buses
Rain on the tree
Rain on the housetops
But not on me

They might manage to change more than the green grass:

Rain on the flowers
Rain on the sea
Rain on the shelter
But not on me

Domain 3: Mathematical development

1   Direction

Help the children's sense of direction!

Photocopy two sheets of page 54 for each child.

Show the children how to get out of each maze using the first sheet, and let them try for themselves on their second sheet.

2   Up and down directions

Use the Incy Wincy Spider rhyme again. The children "do" the climbing **up** and washed **down** actions.

They could also pretend to climb **up** to the slide and slide **down** to the floor.

Domain 4: Knowledge and understanding of the world

1   **View on the world**

Tell the children to pretend they are looking out of the window at a busy street. It is a rainy day. What can they see? (People with raincoats, hats, umbrellas; puddles; wet dog; raindrops on the window.)

Next, tell the children to pretend to be looking out on a sunny day. What can they see? (The sun. Blue sky. People in summer clothes – shorts, summer dresses, t-shirts. Sun hats. The clear shop windows. A baby with a parasol over his pushchair.)

2   **Water project**

Use this story if you are doing a project on Water or the Seasons.

- What happens to water when it is very cold?
- What happens to water when it is very hot?

Photocopy page 56. Younger children can look at the images as you talk; older children can write "water" on the drip from the tap, the ice cube and the steam.

3   **Ice**

You could get ice from the fridge and see how it melts. In winter you could show them ice on the puddles. You could flavour the water with orange juice and make each child an ice-lolly.

- What do we need water for? (To drink, wash, clean, swim in, sail on, etc. To water the grass and the plants.)

The children could illustrate some of these uses with a series of pictures.

Find the Water

Domain 5: Physical development

Funfair actions to music

The children could pretend to be at the funfair. Play some suitable music while the children pretend to go round on a galloping horse on a roundabout; climb up to the top of a slide and slide down; pair with another child to make a see-saw.

Domain 6: Creative development

1   Acting out the story

The children can work in groups of three. One child is Dad, one is Tom, one child is Molly.

Tom waves goodbye and says he is off to the bouncy slide. Dad looks under the bonnet of his car. Molly slips off and goes on the roundabout. Molly runs to the tent out of the rain.

(The teacher reads out the lost child announcement.)

Molly searches for Dad. She sees Tom climbing up near the top of the slide. She runs to the slide. Tom slides down. He hugs Molly. He phones Dad. "Dad, she's here at the slide with me."

Dad runs to the slide. He gives Molly a hug. "I was worried."

"I won't get lost again," Molly says.

2   My house

Have the children draw a picture of their house. Help them to write the correct number on the door. They can draw a picture of themselves standing by the house. Help them to write their name under this child. Older children, with your help, may be able to copy their address onto the page.

Co-operative poster activity

Make a rainy day and a sunny day poster.

Draw a black cloud with some raindrops at the top of one big sheet and a sun with white clouds at the top of the other sheet. The children draw one thing from each of these lists:

Rain	Sunshine
A man with an umbrella	A man wearing shorts
A woman with an umbrella	A woman in a flowery dress
A man in a raincoat and rain-hat	A child with a sun-hat
A woman in a raincoat and rain-hat	A boy with an ice cream
A child in a raincoat and rain-hat	A woman with sunglasses
A wet dog	A girl with an ice cream
A puddle with a duck on it	A woman on a bench, sunbathing, eyes shut, face towards the sun
What else?	A man in an open-top car
	What else?

Now choose one picture by each child to be stuck on the correct poster.

Chapter 5

Birthday Balloons

Teacher's Notes

Theme Five: **Imagination; Pretend Friends.** Young children often find it difficult to distinguish between the real and the "pretend". We need to encourage the development of the creative imagination while also developing their understanding of the real/unreal distinction.

Associated Values: **Creativity; Kindness.** We can encourage children to use their imagination in creative ways – being creative in play, ideas, pictures, stories etc. (Where children create a "pretend" friend, we can respect this – recognising there is a need for comfort and security, as a younger child finds in a comfort blanket or favourite soft toy.)

Associated Emotions: **Satisfaction; Affection.** Children can derive considerable satisfaction from creating something – from the development of a skilful imagination (when children create a pretend friend they will usually feel strong affection for it/him/her).

Associated Relationships: The theme and story exhibit relationships with the **self** (one's imagination or creative self); with **others** (an understanding Mum and playschool friends). In addition the story shows how a child can have a relationship with a "pretend" other.

Early Years Teaching

Early Years Experiences:	This theme of **Imagination** is closely allied with the sixth foundation area – **Creative Development**. Children can be creative in making something of their own, and they begin to develop a desire (and increasing skills) to "create" to the best of their ability. This particular story readily taps into early years experiences of birthday parties, and of "pretending".
Early Years Topics:	This fifth chapter contains relevant material for teachers exploring the following topics: **Ourselves** (Likes and Dislikes. Friends (pretend friends). Imagination); **Toys/Play** (Old and new toys. Favourite toys. Presents. Let's pretend games); **Colour** (Balloons make a useful focus for colour and counting).
Early Years Skills:	**The Six Learning Domains.** Pages 68–70 provide learning games and activities for each of the early years foundation areas. These are all linked to the story and its associated theme.

Session Plan: Relationships

This timescale is provisional only. Feel free to "go with" the children's own pace. Above all, adapt the material to suit your particular group of children. There is a big difference in teaching a group of three-year-old children and a group of five-year-olds, or a mixed age group, and between teaching one or two children or a bigger group.

1   Introduce the story   *2–5 minutes*
    Introduce the theme   *3–5 minutes*

2   The story   *5–10 minutes*

The teacher shows the illustration and suggested objects before reading the story. The story can be retold in several sessions, to be followed by a different learning activity each time. Children enjoy listening to a familiar story and may absorb new aspects each time.

3   Talking about the story; associated stories and rhymes   *5–10 minutes*

The teacher uses some of the questions and discussion points given, stimulating the children to talk about the story/theme. Additionally, there are further story, poem and song suggestions provided, and a relevant traditional poem or nursery rhyme.

4   Learning games and activities   *5–30 minutes*

For each story, learning activities in each of the **six** learning domains are provided. There is also a "co-operative poster" to be made and/or enjoyed.

Total time   *20–60 minutes*

1   INTRODUCE THE STORY AND THEME

To introduce the story

- The teacher tells the children that the story is about Sam's birthday party.
- Sam has a pretend friend called Spikey (a hedgehog).
- Perhaps the teacher can have some balloons for the children to play with and/or a toy hedgehog to show them.

To introduce the theme

- The teacher asks the children about their favourite toys. Does anyone have a pretend friend to play with?
- The teacher and children can also talk about birthdays and birthday parties.
- Sam wanted a red birthday party. See if the children have any ideas for a different or unusual or special birthday party.

Additional points

- Many stories are pretend. This story is about a pretend Sam and a pretend party – as well as about Sam's pretend friend. See if the children can begin to see the difference between a pretend friend and a real one. (No one else can see the pretend friend; everyone can see "real" friends.)

THE BASIC STORY:

Birthday Balloons

It was Sam's birthday. He had a new red swing.

"Spikey wants my party to be red, like the swing," he told his mummy.
Spikey was Sam's pretend friend – a hedgehog with red shoes.
Mummy made a red jelly and a red fire engine cake, and Sam's friends came to the party.
"We can't see Spikey," they said.
A balloon burst. "Spikey did that," said Sam. "With his spikes".
One by one the party balloons burst. The children laughed. "It's Spikey," they said.
The children had a turn on Sam's new swing. They sang Happy Birthday to Sam.
At bedtime Sam said, "That was a great party, Mummy. And Spikey liked it too."

Birthday Balloons

Birthday Balloons

Sam woke up and peeped out between the bedroom curtains. Yes! A new red swing was in the garden. He rushed downstairs, his face lit up with excitement.

"Happy Birthday, Sam," said Mummy.

"It's Spikey's birthday too," Sam said.

"Happy Birthday, Spikey," said Mummy.

"Spikey wants red food at our party," Sam reminded her.

"Yes. To match his shoes."

Mummy couldn't see Spikey but she knew all about Sam's pretend friend. He was a talking hedgehog with red shoes on all his four little feet.

In the afternoon Grace, Thomas and Harry came for the party. They were Sam's friends at playschool. On a red tablecloth Mummy had put a big pizza covered in slices of red tomato, a red bowl full of chips, a red wobbly jelly and red ice cream. In the centre of the table was a red fire-engine birthday cake. About ten balloons floated round the room. Sam jumped up and down with excitement.

Sam, Grace, Thomas and Harry sat down at the table and ate the red food. The children sang Happy Birthday and Sam smiled so much he almost couldn't blow out the candles on his cake.

"Spikey wanted a red birthday cake," Sam told his friends. "He's my talking hedgehog. He's sitting on this chair and eating jelly."

"He likes jelly," said Mummy.

Grace looked at Sam's mummy. She looked at Sam. She looked at the empty chair.

"But there's no hedgehog there," she said.

"He's invisible," said Sam. "Except to me."

"But there's no hedgehog there," said Thomas. "Not really."

Sam began to feel upset.

"Is he just pretend?" said Harry.

"Yes, but he's my real pretend friend," Sam explained.

"But there's no hedgehog there," said Harry. "No real hedgehog, I mean."

"Now you've hurt Spikey's feelings," shouted Sam.

There was a loud bang and everyone jumped. A balloon had burst.

"Who did that?" said Grace.

"No one touched it," said Thomas.

"It was Spikey," said Sam. "He's cross and he burst it."

Another balloon went pop.

"We won't buy this kind again," said Dad, looking at the packet.

"It's Spikey," said Sam, cheering up. "He's bursting them one by one with his spikes."

"Wow," said Grace. "With his spikes."

The children watched the balloons, wondering which one Spikey would burst next. They tried to guess.

"The red one."

"No, the blue one."

It was exciting waiting for the bang and each time a balloon burst it made the children laugh. They had great fun.

When all the balloons had burst Harry said to Sam, "Come on. Let's play out on your new swing. Spikey can come too."

"Yes," Sam agreed.

Everyone had a good time in the garden.

At bedtime, after Sam's friends had gone home, Mummy said, "Did you enjoy your birthday, Sam?"

"Yes," said Sam. "And Spikey did too."

3 TALKING ABOUT THE STORY

The teacher and children talk about the story:

- What did Sam have in the garden for his birthday present?
- What was the name of Sam's pretend friend?
- What kind of animal was Spikey?
- What colour were Spikey's shoes?
- What is your favourite colour?
- What did Sam have for his birthday tea party?
- What is your favourite food?
- What made the children believe in Spikey?
- Did Sam enjoy his party?

Associated stories, songs, poems and nursery rhymes

Stories

Smith the Lonely Hedgehog by Althea (Dinosaur Publications)
Magic Balloons (in the Puddle Lane series) by Sheila McCullagh (Ladybird Books)

Songs

Holly the Hedgehog (in *Ralph McTell's Alphabet Zoo Songbook*) (Ward Lock Educational)

Poems and nursery rhymes

The Hedgehog (in *Rhyme Time* edited by Barbara Ireson) (Beaver Books)
Boot the Hedgehog (in *The Squirrel in Town and Other Native Poems* by Stanley Cook *et al.*) (Blackie)
The Hedgehog (in *Seeing and Doing: An Anthology of Songs and Poems*) (Mammoth)
Happy Birthday Card by Tony Robinson (in *A Very First Poetry Book* edited by John Foster) OUP

Happy Birthday to You

Happy Birthday to you
Happy Birthday to you
Happy Birthday dear Sam
Happy Birthday to you

Birth Days

Monday's child is fair of face
Tuesday's child is full of grace
Wednesday's child is full of woe
Thursday's child has far to go
Friday's child is loving and giving
Saturday's child works hard for his living
And the child that is born on the Sabbath day is bonny and blithe and good and gay.

(I always feel bad for Wednesday's children and substitute something, e.g. Wednesday's child can tie a bow.)

Note: You can find other examples of stories, songs, poems which link to the story or theme – i.e. they could be about birthdays or pretend friends or balloons or hedgehogs.

4   LEARNING GAMES AND ACTIVITIES

Domain 1: Personal, social and emotional development

1   Circle Time game/question
Pretend Friend

Let's play an imagination game. Go round the circle asking the children to "imagine" a pretend friend. What are they? (A hedgehog? A little girl? A dog? A lion?) What is their name?

Tell me something about ... (Use the name given.) (She wears a red hat. She likes fish fingers. He is very good at drawing.)

2   Circle Time talk
Talk about friendship. Why do we all need friends? What is a good friend like? Why might we have a pretend friend? (To play with when our friends are not there. To tell things to. To stop us feeling lonely or anxious e.g. at night time.) How many of you have a pretend friend? What do we call it when we create/make up something or someone? (Using our imagination.)

Domain 2: Communication, language and literacy

1   Language
In pairs get the children to describe their made-up "pretend" friend.

After this the children can draw the pretend friend. Use these portraits to have the children describe the pretend friend to the class. Who/what is s/he? What does s/he wear? What does s/he look like? What is s/he good at? What does s/he like/dislike? Is s/he kind? Anything else?

2   Adjectives
Follow up the work on "pretend friends" by holding up objects for which the children can supply adjectives. ("Tell me what this is like. What colour? What else?") Hold up a ball. (Round. Red.) Hold up a teddy bear. (Brown. Furry. Cuddly.)

Domain 3: Mathematical development

1   Five balloons
Make a poster-sized drawing of five balloons. Ask the children in turn to come and point to the colours: red, yellow, blue, green, black. Count the balloons with the children.

- How many red balloons are there? (One)
- How many red plus yellow balloons? (Two)

2   Sizes
Collect boxes with lids of all sizes. Give each child a box or a lid and have them find their match and put box and lid together.

Take each box in turn and ask the children to think of something the right size to fit in it. Your comments will guide the children without discouraging suggestions. ("That is a good idea, Jenny, that would be just the right size." "It would need to be a small hedgehog, Jenny. Perhaps this box would be better to fit a hedgehog.)

Domain 4: Knowledge and understanding of the world

1   Introduce the word/idea of electricity

Rub a balloon on your clothes to create static electricity and stick it on the wall. Let the children do this too. They will be very interested. Use the opportunity to say electricity also powers our lights. Switch the lights on and off. And the television. What else? You could also show some magnets in action (magnets are already familiar to many children from fridge-magnets).

2   Hedgehog

If the grass seeds on the potatoes (Chapter 3) have grown, the children can paint or draw on eyes and nose (or make a hole in the potato and push through some foil to make the nose). You can then explain to the children that hedgehogs' prickles prevent them from being eaten by other animals.

Domain 5: Physical development

Let the children have some fun exercise with the balloons, batting them to keep them in the air, batting to each other in pairs.

Have the children crouch as small as they can and pretend to be balloons blowing up. They get bigger and bigger, saying these words:

Blow and blow
I grow and grow
Stretch and stretch and
I'm the first
To stretch and stretch and
BURST!

(They can "burst" with a big, wide-armed jump at the end.)

Domain 6: Creative development

1   Printing

Mix some red, yellow, green, blue and black paint in separate pots. Add a little wallpaper paste to make it thick for printing. Cut some oval potatoes in half across their length. (This will give a "balloon" shape.) The children can use the red, yellow, green, blue and black to **print** five balloon shapes. They can draw in the string.

2   Magic picture

Provide sturdy white paper for each child. Using leftover paint from their printing, the children choose two or three colours to dab onto their paper. Fold the paper. Encourage the children to move their finger around the folded paper. Open the paper to find their lovely symmetrical abstract picture.

This simple way of making a symmetrical picture will enable the children to experience the "magic" of creating a lovely picture and the enjoyment of colour.

3   Birthday card

The children can turn their magic picture into a birthday card. They can write HAPPY BIRTHDAY on the inside and draw a birthday picture on the front.

4   **Co-operative poster activity**
    Peeping faces
    Cut up potatoes, carrots and turnips. Together, the children print onto a poster-sized
    sheet of paper. They could then each choose one of the "circles" and draw a face on it
    – perhaps with hair or a hat or glasses or a beard. These faces will "peep" out of the
    remaining blank prints.

Chapter 6

One Red Spade

Teacher's Notes

Theme Six:	**Friendship.** Young children love to have someone to play with. They need peer relationships/friendships. They can begin to learn about making friends, being a good friend, and making up after a quarrel.
Associated Values:	**Empathy; Co-operation.** Children can be very attached to their friend(s) and this affection encourages kindness and the development of empathy. Peer relationships also teach children how to co-operate – that friendship demands give and take.
Associated Emotions:	**Affection.** Because friendship is important we should encourage children's friendships and respect their peer relationships. They will learn that when we care for someone they can hurt us, but that without friends we are lonely. We share affection and kindness in a good friendship.
Associated Relationships:	The theme of **friendship** is at the heart of this story. Manjit makes a friend, enjoys the friendship and falls out with her friend and is sad. Her own gesture of generosity heals the breach. Thus there is an exploration of Manjit's relationship with Louisa and the influence of the relationship on Manjit's own feelings and actions.

Early Years Teaching

Early Years Experiences	Friends are an important part of a child's world. Most children will have experienced "falling out" with a friend and "I'm not your friend" is a significant emotional response!

Early Years Topics   This theme (Friendship) is an aspect of other chapters and stories (e.g. Chapter 3, Akram and Joe; Chapter 5, Sam and Spikey; Chapter 7, Joshua and his baby brother). However, this story directly explores the relationship of friendship and quarrelling, and it links with early years topics on Ourselves and Others and, indeed, is sufficiently significant to count as an early years topic in its own right.

Early Years Skills: **The Six Learning Domains.** Pages 79–81 provide learning games and activities for each of the early years foundation areas. These are all linked to the story and its associated theme.

Session Plan: Friends

This timescale is provisional only. Feel free to "go with" the children's own pace. Above all, adapt the material to suit your particular group of children. There is a big difference in teaching a group of three-year-old children and a group of five-year-olds, or a mixed age group, and between teaching one or two children or a bigger group.

1   **Introduce the story**   *2–5 minutes*
     Introduce the theme   *3–5 minutes*

2   **The story**   *5–10 minutes*
     The teacher shows the illustration and suggested objects before reading the story. The story can be retold in several sessions, to be followed by a different learning activity each time. Children enjoy listening to a familiar story and may absorb new aspects each time.

3   **Talking about the story; associated stories and rhymes**   *5–10 minutes*
     The teacher uses some of the questions and discussion points given, stimulating the children to talk about the story/theme. Additionally, there are further story, poem and song suggestions provided, and a relevant traditional poem or nursery rhyme.

4   **Learning games and activities**   *5–30 minutes*
     For each story, learning activities in each of the **six** learning domains are provided. There is also a "co-operative poster" to be made and/or enjoyed.

| Total time | *20–60 minutes* |

1 INTRODUCE THE STORY AND THEME

To introduce the story

- The teacher tells the children that the story is about Manjit, who falls out with her best friend, Louisa.
- The teacher could show the children a bucket and spade and a hair scrunchie.
- The teacher shows the children the illustrations of the story.

To introduce the theme

- The teacher asks the children the name of one of their friends. They talk about these friends.
- How can we make friends?
- Why do we need friends?
- Have you ever fallen out with your friend?
- How did you become friends again?

Additional points

- Be aware if you have shy or lonely children in the class, so that they are not embarrassed in the discussion.
- Perhaps this theme could be an opportunity to help them to make friends. (Choose their partners carefully in the "get to know someone" activity on page 79.)

2 THE BASIC STORY:

One Red Spade

Manjit was playing in the sand corner. She made a sand-pie. Louisa helped Manjit. They became friends.

One day Manjit and Louisa both wanted the red spade. They quarrelled. Louisa grabbed the spade.

"You mean thing," said Manjit.

All day Manjit and Louisa did not talk to each other. Manjit had no one to play with. She was sad.

At home time Mummy gave Manjit two pink hair scrunchies. Manjit saw Louisa looking sad.

Manjit gave one of the hair scrunchies to Louisa.

Manjit and Louisa were friends again. They were happy.

2 THE ADVANCED STORY:

One Red Spade

The Story

One Red Spade

It was Manjit's first day at playschool. At first she held tight to Mummy's hand, but when she noticed the sand corner, she ran there to play.

There were buckets and spades in the sand corner. Manjit picked up the red spade. She filled a bucket with sand and made a perfect sand-pie.

"That's a good one," said a smiling girl. "What's your name? I'm Louisa."

Louisa helped Manjit to decorate the sand-pie. They pressed in coloured stones which glowed like jewels. Side by side, Manjit and Louisa admired it together.

"I'll be your friend," Louisa said.

Every day at playschool Manjit and Louisa played together. They sat together, they talked together, they worked together and they shared things. Until one day, playing at the sand corner, Manjit and Louisa both reached for the red spade.

"I want the red one," Manjit said, holding the flat part.

"I want it too," said Louisa, holding onto the handle.

The two friends began to tug for the spade.

Manjit held on hard, but Louisa had the handle and could pull harder. Slowly she tugged the spade from Manjit's grasp.

"Ouch," said Manjit, rubbing her hands together. "That hurt. You mean thing."

"Mean yourself," said Louisa, turning her back on Manjit. She began to dig with the red spade and Manjit walked away.

All the rest of the day Manjit and Louisa ignored one another. At milk time Manjit sat by herself. At break time she stood by herself. At art time she had no one to talk to while she was painting her picture and no one to show it to when it was finished. Manjit felt sad. It was lonely not to have a best friend.

At home time Manjit ran to Mummy as soon as she arrived.

"Look," said Mummy. "Aunty Azra sent you two hair scrunchies."

The scrunchies were pink and sparkly.

Louisa was looking at Manjit. She looked sad.

Manjit held out the scrunchies. "You can have one, Louisa," she said. Louisa smiled.

"Thank you Manjit. It's lovely. Let's both wear them tomor-row and pretend to be twins."

Manjit nodded. She felt happy again.

3 TALKING ABOUT THE STORY

The teacher and children talk about the story:

- Why did Manjit hold tight to Mummy's hand?
- Where did Manjit go and play?
- What did she make?
- Who helped Manjit to decorate the sand-pie?
- How did they make it look nice?
- Why did Manjit and Louisa quarrel?
- Why was Manjit sad?
- What did Mummy give Manjit?
- How did Manjit make up her quarrel with Louisa?
- What did Louisa say?

Associated stories, songs, poems and nursery rhymes

Stories

Do You Want to be My Friend? by Eric Carle (Picture Puffin)
Friends by Althea (Dinosaur Publications)
Best Friends by Steven Kellogg (Hutchinson)
We are Best Friends by Aliki (Bodley Head)

Songs

Take Care of a Friend (in *Every Colour Under the Sun*) (Ward Lock Educational)
When I Needed a Neighbour (in *Someone's Singing Lord* by Beatrice Harrop) (A&C Black)
What Are Friends Like? (in *Sing, Say and Move* edited by Jill McWilliam) (Scripture Union)
Oh, I am Playing All Alone (in *Gently into Music* by Mary Yorke) (Cambridge University Press)
It's Not Much Fun (in *Something to Think About* edited by Paddy Bechely) (BBC, 1982)

Poems and nursery rhymes

Small Quarrel (in *Please Mrs Butler* by Allan Ahlberg) (Puffin)
The Best of Friends edited by Tony Bradman (in the Poems for Me series) (Blackie)
I Had No Friends At All by John Kitching (in *A Very First Poetry Book* edited by John Foster) (OUP)
Friends by Margaret Goldthorpe (in *Poems for Circle Time and Literacy Hour*) (LDA)
New Friend by Margaret Goldthorpe (in *Poems for Circle Time and Literacy Hour*) (LDA)

There are surprisingly few traditional rhymes about friendship, quarrelling or making up but Bobby Shafto matches the sand-pie/seaside element in the story.

Bobby Shafto

Bobby Shafto went to sea
Silver buckles on his knee
When he comes home he'll marry me
Pretty Bobby Shafto.

Note: You can find other examples of stories, songs and poems which link to the story or theme – i.e. they could be about friends, quarrels, the seaside, gifts.

4 LEARNING GAMES AND ACTIVITIES

Domain 1: Personal, social and emotional development

1   Circle Time game/question

Go round the circle and ask each child for one nice thing they like about their friend.

Next, ask the children to think about a time when they quarrelled with their friend. What was it about? How did they feel?

We all quarrel from time to time but it is good to know how to make up.

How can we make friends again? (We could smile at our friends. We could say sorry. We could say we didn't mean it and won't do it again. We could start to play with them again.)

2   Circle Time talk

Go round the circle and ask what do you like to do/play with your friend(s)? How does your friend help you? How do you help your friend? Talk with the children about what they could do to be friendly, helpful and kind to a new boy or girl who had just joined the playschool. (Play with him/her at playtime. Talk to him/her at lunchtime. Share with him/her. Show him/her where things are – coat peg, toilet, crayons. Offer to be his/her partner in a "class" activity.)

Domain 2: Communication, language and literacy

1   Get to know someone new

Pair the children with a child they don't know very well. Ask them to take turns to "interview" each other – to find out as much as they can, and to see if they can find something they have in common. Where do they live? What toys/games/food do they like? When is their birthday? Where is their favourite place? Do they have a pet?

2   Ingredients

Show the children an eggcup, a tablespoon, a teaspoon. Show them what a pinch is (e.g. a pinch of salt).

Tell the children this "recipe":
Take an eggcup of smiles
A tablespoon of funny jokes
A teaspoon of kindness
A pinch of sharing
To make ONE GOOD FRIEND.

Each child must think of four other ingredients to "make a friend". (Fun, caring, listening, understanding, etc. Draw on the things they said in Circle Time to help them find "friend" qualities.) For example:

Take an eggcup of fun
A tablespoon of understanding
A teaspoon of laughing
To make ONE GOOD FRIEND.

Domain 3: Mathematical development

Sharing: A lot and a few

Have a large number of several objects (buttons, counters, crayons, marbles ...).
Give pairs of children a heap (say 20) to share between them: "One for you, one for me."
Have you (each) got a lot or a few? (A lot.)
Link up the pairs. The four children divide the joined heaps between them.
Have you (each) got a lot or a few? (A lot.)
Link up eight children. Give them only one heap to share between them.
Have you (each) got a lot or a few? (A few.)

Domain 4: Knowledge and understanding of the world

Pictures

Have the children draw a picture of two friends who are playing together. Perhaps they are playing catch with a ball.

Have the children draw a picture of three friends playing together. Perhaps they are skipping, two turning the rope while one skips in the middle.

Talk to the children about what other activities need two people or benefit from co-operation, e.g. wrapping a parcel – one holds the paper down and the other puts on the sticky tape. (The children could practice a co-operative activity.)

Domain 5: Physical development

Running and jumping together

Young children love to run and jump and can do these fun activities together.

Have the children in pairs. The two children must hold hands and jump together – 1, 2, 3, 4, 5. After some practice each pair links with another pair. Can four children jump together – 1, 2, 3, 4, 5?

Have the children form new pairs. The two children link arms and must run round until the music stops, when they must both stop immediately. One child stands still while his/her friend must hop around him. The still child says, "HOP, HOP, HOP" and the hopping child hops until the still child cries "STOP". ("HOP. HOP. HOP. HOP. STOP!")

The children change places and repeat the game.

Domain 6: Creative development

1   A story

Make up a class story about a new girl who, like Manjit, joined the playgroup and made a friend.

One day a new girl joined the playschool. She was called .... (The children decide on a name.) She didn't know anyone there. She had no one to play with until ... (What happened? Who spoke to her? What did they say? What did they play?) ... was happy until she fell out with her new friend. (What happened? Why did they quarrel?) ... was sad. She had no one to play with again. (How did they make up and become friends again?)

Having accepted some suggestions from the children, you then "tell" them *their* story.

Repeat the process with a story about a new boy.

2   **Happy face**
Give each child a paper plate to paint a happy friendly face on.

3   **Bookmarks**
Give each child two pieces of card – about 5cm × 13cm. (i.e. bookmark shape). Using stick-on stars and other shapes they can decorate their bookmarks. They could cut a pointed end (optional). One bookmark is for the child and can be taken home and one is for the child to give a friend or relative (i.e. someone they want to give it to!).

You could follow up making the bookmarks with a library/reading session. The children could choose a book. (Perhaps they can find one about two friends.)

Co-operative poster activity

Friends

- Have the children stick their happy (plate) face onto a big sheet of paper.
- Mix up some paint in appropriate shades of pale pinks and browns. Have each child draw round their own hand and another child's hand. Each child paints these two hands, trying to match the skin tone – their own skin tone for their own hand and the skin tone of the child whose hand they drew for the other hand.
- Each child sticks the two hands so that they touch – finding a space between the faces.

Chapter 7

The New Baby

Teacher's Notes

Theme Seven: **Family Relationships and Jealousy.** Young children usually feel some degree of jealousy of a new baby in the family – babies inevitably take up much "carer" attention. They need reassurance that such feelings are understandable and much reassurance that they are still loved just as much as before. Ideally they can become involved in "caring" for the baby – thus developing their own capacity to care for the more vulnerable.

Associated Values: **Family Friendship; Care; Protectiveness.** We can be good friends with our brothers and sisters. (This follows well from Chapter 6.)

Associated Emotions: **From Jealousy to Care/Love.** We can help to prepare children for the new arrival – helping them to be more prepared for the attention/help that a baby needs. We can prepare them for the jealous feelings they may have, but also teach them about a new baby's total dependence, vulnerability and needs.

Associated Relationships: **Family relationships** are important. The teacher must work with an awareness that there are different kinds of family. Some children may live with grandma or a foster family, etc. What counts is loving, caring relationships. (Sadly, a minority of children do not have this care and may manifest this and need help.)

Early Years Teaching

Early Years Experiences: A child's carer(s) is/are at the centre of a child's world and many children will have experienced jealousy in having to share the carer's attention and love – especially with the arrival of a new sibling.

Early Years Topics: This theme and story links with important early years topics: **Ourselves** (Our Emotions; Our Family); Others (Relationship with siblings and with younger/weaker children; Families).

Early Years Skills: **The Six Learning Domains.** Pages 92–3 provide learning games and activities for each of the early years foundation areas. These are all linked to the story and its associated theme.

Session Plan: Families; jealousy; care

This timescale is provisional only. Feel free to "go with" the children's own pace. Above all, adapt the material to suit your particular group of children. There is a big difference in teaching a group of three-year-old children and a group of five-year-olds, or a mixed age group, and between teaching one or two children or a bigger group.

1 Introduce the story   *2–5 minutes*

Introduce the theme   *3–5 minutes*

2 The story   *5–10 minutes*

The teacher shows the illustration and suggested objects before reading the story. The story can be retold in several sessions, to be followed by a different learning activity each time. Children enjoy listening to a familiar story and may absorb new aspects each time.

3 Talking about the story; associated stories and rhymes   *5–10 minutes*

The teacher uses some of the questions and discussion points given, stimulating the children to talk about the story/theme. Additionally, there are further story, poem and song suggestions provided, and a relevant traditional poem or nursery rhyme.

4 Learning games and activities   *5–30 minutes*

For each story, learning activities in each of the **six** learning domains are provided. There is also a "co-operative poster" to be made and/or enjoyed.

Total time | *20–60 minutes*

1 INTRODUCE THE STORY AND THEME

To introduce the story

- The teacher tells the children that the story is about Joshua, who is jealous of his new baby brother but comes to care about him.
- You could show the children some pictures of babies to show all the care they need: feeding, rocking to sleep, burping, bathing, dressing, etc.
- Show the children the illustrations for the story.

To introduce the theme

- The teacher says that most of us sometimes experience being jealous – especially of a young baby. She asks: have any of you felt jealous? Who/what were you jealous of? How did it feel?
- The teacher reminds children that they need less help than a helpless baby but they are still loved.

Additional points

- Talk about "families". Say that some children have a mummy and daddy to look after them. Some children have a grandma or aunty. These are all families because they live together and help each other.

2 THE BASIC STORY:

The New Baby

Mummy had a new baby, a brother for Joshua.

"Isn't he beautiful?" she said.

Joshua didn't think baby Darren was beautiful. He was bald and he cried a lot.

Everyone fussed over the new baby and gave him presents. Joshua felt left out and cross. When no one was looking he pinched his new brother. Baby Darren cried and cried. Mummy was worried and Joshua felt bad.

The next day Joshua was given a present from Darren – a new boat.

"Thank you, Darren," he said. Darren smiled at Joshua.

"His first smile and it was for you," said Mum.

"He looks nice when he smiles," said Joshua.

Joshua felt happy. He and his new brother would be friends.

2 THE ADVANCED STORY:

The New Baby

The New Baby

Mummy was telling Joshua a story. He wriggled about on her knees. These days there wasn't enough room. Mummy was having a baby and her tummy was big. In the story a boy called Jack had three wishes.

"What would you wish for?" Mum said.

"A new boat," said Joshua.

"Not a new brother?"

"No, a new boat."

The next day Dad drove Mummy to the hospital and Grandma came to look after Joshua. The day after that Mummy brought the baby home.

She let Joshua hold his new brother.

"He's called Darren. Isn't he beautiful?"

The baby had wrinkles, a droopy mouth and no hair.

"Not really," Joshua said.

Aunty Safina came to see the new baby. She brought him a teddy bear. She held him in her arms.

"You are a beautiful baby," she said.

Aunty Val came to see the new baby. She brought him a blue coat. She held him in her arms.

"You are a beautiful baby," she said.

Aunty Marcia came to see the new baby. She brought him a soft blanket. She held him in her arms.

"You are a beautiful baby," she said.

Joshua felt left out and grumpy.

"You are a bad baby," he whispered.

The baby cried whenever he was hungry. Joshua hated the sound of the wailing cry. One day when Mum wasn't looking, he pinched his new brother. The baby cried louder than ever before. Mum rushed to pick him up. She looked very worried.

That night Joshua couldn't get to sleep. He could hear the baby crying and crying. "Maybe it's all my fault", he thought.

The next day Mum gave Joshua a big parcel.

"It's from Darren," she said.

Joshua tore off the paper. Inside was a new toy boat. He went to Darren's cot and looked in.

"Thank you, Darren," he said.

Darren looked at Joshua and gave a sudden, big smile.

"His first smile, and it was for you," said Mum.

"I know. It means he wants to be my friend. He looks nice when he smiles," said Joshua, feeling happy. He sat on Mum's knee. These days there was plenty of room.

"Tell me the story about the three wishes," he said.

3 TALKING ABOUT THE STORY

The teacher and children talk about the story:

- What was the name of the new baby?
- Did Joshua like Darren at first?
- Why did Joshua feel left out and cross?
- What bad thing did Joshua do to make Darren cry?
- What present did Darren give to Joshua?
- Why was Joshua happy in the end?
- Why do you think people bring gifts for a new baby? (Babies need many things; it's their first birthday; to welcome them into the family.)

Associated stories, songs, poems and nursery rhymes

Stories

A Baby Sister for Frances by Russell Hoban (Picture Puffin)
Jenny's Baby Brother by Peter Smith (in the Picture Lions series) (Collins)
My Baby Brother Ned by Sumiko (Heinemann)
New Big Sister by Debi Gliori (Walker Books)

Songs

How Many People Live In Your House? (in *Tinder-box: Assembly Book*) (A&C Black)
There's Room Enough for You (in *Every Colour Under the Sun*) (Ward Lock Educational)
We Will Take Care of You (in *Every Colour Under the Sun*) (Ward Lock Educational)

Poems and nursery rhymes

Our Family (in *The Mad Family* edited by Tony Bradman) (Young Puffin)

Hush-a-bye-baby

Hush-a-bye baby on the tree top
When the wind blows the cradle will rock;
When the bough breaks the cradle will fall
Down will come baby, cradle and all.

Bye baby bunting

Bye, baby bunting,
Daddy's gone a hunting
Gone to get a rabbit skin
To wrap the baby bunting in.

("Bunting" is an old form of endearment.)

Rock-a-bye baby

Rock-a-bye baby,
Thy cradle is green,
Father's a nobleman,
Mother's a queen.
And Betty's a lady,
And wears a gold ring,
And Johnny's a drummer,
And drums for the King.

When I Was Young (in *Please Mrs Butler* by Allan Ahlberg) (Puffin)

Note: You can find other examples of stories, songs, poems which link to the story or theme – i.e. they could be about a new baby, brothers and sisters, families, caring, gifts.

4 LEARNING GAMES AND ACTIVITIES

Domain 1: Personal, social and emotional development

1   Circle Time games/questions

- Go round the circle and say: "Tell me the names of your brothers and sisters." Or, for only children: "What name would you choose if you had a brother or sister?" Go round the circle and ask what the children could do when they were a baby. (Cry, drink milk, smile, sleep.) Ask what they can do **now** that a baby can't yet do.

2   Circle Time talk

- Who has a baby brother or sister? Did you feel jealous at first? How should we behave towards smaller children and babies? How can you help with the baby?
- We were all babies once. What do we need to grow up big and strong? (Milk, someone to look after us, a cot, a pram, toys, etc.)

Domain 2: Communication, language and literacy

1   Baby vocabulary

Have the children identify baby equipment. (You could use a catalogue as a source of pictures: bottle; cot; pushchair; bath, etc.)

2   Adjectives

Hold up baby objects and have the children supply adjectives (e.g. a rattle – blue, noisy).

Domain 3: Mathematical development

There was once a big family with so many children that five slept in one bed. Do the "roll over" rhyme – holding up five fingers until there are none. Second time round the children join in.

> *There were five in the bed and the little one said,*
> *"Roll over, roll over."*
> *So they all rolled over and one fell out.*
> *There were four in the bed and the little one said,*
> *"Roll over, roll over."*
> *So they all rolled over and one fell out ... etc.*

Domain 4: Knowledge and understanding of the world

Toy teacher

Use this as an opportunity to reinforce the children's learning from any recent work. For example – name, address, telephone number from Chapter 3.

Ask the children to bring in a favourite teddy bear or doll or Action Man. (Children who forget can choose one of the playschool toys.) Explain to the children that they will be a Toy Teacher for the day. Begin with the item to be revised (as in the example above). Re-teach the children. The children pass it on to "teach" their toy.

They can continue to "teach" their toy throughout the day.

Note: Since we remember things better once we have told/taught them to someone else, and children love to take on a grown-up persona, this is a good way to reinforce key learning, and one that you could deploy on a regular basis (e.g. every Wednesday could be designated Toy Day).

(Tell the children that they can be the Toy Teacher every day when they go home.)

Domain 5: Physical development

Baby movements and progress

Have the children lie down.

First a baby learns to lift her head. (The children do this.) Up. Down. Up. Down. Up. Down.

Next a baby learns how to sit up. (The children do this.)

Next a baby learns how to crawl. (The children do this.)

Next a baby learns how to walk. (The children walk – pretending to be unsteady like a baby.)

But we are big and can run ... we can jump ... we can hop ...

Domain 6: Creative development

Make a family

● Collect cardboard tubes from toilet rolls and kitchen paper. Give one to each child.

● Help the children to draw a face on the top half of the tube. Stick on wool, felt, cotton wool and coloured paper to make hair or moustaches and clothes. Some children can make a daddy, others a mummy, others a boy or a girl or a baby, or a grandma or grandpa, or even a dog. These tube people can be grouped into several families of different sizes and structure.

● Give the children an A3 sheet of card. Allow the children to choose a picture from your card collection. If they have a baby brother or sister they can choose a "baby" picture e.g. teddy bear. Children with no baby can choose to make the gift for someone else e.g. Mummy and choose a non-baby picture e.g. flowers.

● The children cut out the picture and glue it in the middle of the card. They could also cut lengths of a different colour of card to "frame" the picture.

● Finally, with your help they make two holes and add ribbon or string for hanging the picture they have made.

Co-operative poster activity

Ask the children to bring in a photo of when they were a baby or very young child – photos that Mummy can spare as they will be used for a class poster. Jumble all the photos together and then have a fun session in which you hold up each picture in turn and the children have to guess who it is. (You must warn the children **not** to speak up when you show their photo.) The children take turns to glue their photo onto the class poster. (You could work out, **with the children**, an age order, i.e. new babies, young children, and glue the pictures in age order to show growth.)

Babies	Children

Chapter 8

Seeing the Sea

Teacher's Notes

Theme Eight:	**Imagination.** This is an opportunity for children to learn that their imagination can be used to prevent boredom. To "make" something (e.g. a picture of the seaside, or a sand-castle at the seaside) or to "make up" a story is fun.
Associated Values:	**Creativity.** We use our imagination when we create something. To create something is valuable for **ourselves** (using skill, getting more skilful, fun) and for **others** (to enjoy our picture or story, etc.)
Associated Emotions:	**Fulfilment** (instead of **boredom**). We feel a sense of satisfaction when we create something good.
Associated Relationships:	Creativity relates **inwardly** (fulfilling our need to create and allowing self-expression) and it relates **outwardly** (making something in the world that enhances the world, either aesthetically or by increasing our understanding).

Early Years Teaching

Early Years Experiences:	Children enjoy both **making things** and "**making things up**" in their play. Like Sophie, they know how **frustrating** it can be if prevented from doing something they long to do, and like Sophie they have all experienced **boredom** ("nothing to do"). Some children will have stayed in a caravan, some will have been to the seaside and all will have experienced heavy rain!

Early Years Topics: This theme and story links with important early years topics: **The Seaside** (Sea. Sand. Activities. Creatures); **Holidays; The Weather** (and Seasons); **Water/Rain.**

Early Years Skills: **The Six Learning Domains.** Pages 103–6 provide learning games and activities for each of the early years foundation areas. These are all linked to the story and its associated theme.

Session Plan: Imagination

This timescale is provisional only. Feel free to "go with" the children's own pace. Above all, adapt the material to suit your particular group of children. There is a big difference in teaching a group of three-year-old children and a group of five-year-olds, or a mixed age group, and between teaching one or two children or a bigger group.

█   Introduce the story   *2–5 minutes*
Introduce the theme   *3–5 minutes*

2   The story   *5–10 minutes*
The teacher shows the illustration and suggested objects before read-ing the story. The story can be retold in several sessions, to be followed by a different learning activity each time. Children enjoy lis-tening to a familiar story and may absorb new aspects each time.

3   Talking about the story; associated stories and rhymes   *5–10 minutes*
The teacher uses some of the questions and discussion points given, stimulating the children to talk about the story/theme. Additionally, there are further story, poem and song suggestions provided, and a rel-evant traditional poem or nursery rhyme.

█   Learning games and activities   *5–30 minutes*
For each story, learning activities in each of the **six** learning domains are provided. There is also a "co-operative poster" to be made and/or enjoyed.

Total time   *20–60 minutes*

1   INTRODUCE THE STORY AND THEME

To introduce the story

- The teacher tells the children that the story is about how Sophie imagines that she goes on a magic carpet to the seaside.
- The teacher shows the children the illustrations to the story.
- The teacher shows the children a pack of cards – especially the Jack of Hearts.
- The teacher could show a seaside poster and identify, with the children, the sea and sand, the boats, people, sandcastles, etc.

To introduce the theme

Sophie imagined she went on the magic carpet. Close your eyes. Now imagine you and your friend are sitting on a red rug. The rug is magic. It rises up in the air. Tell it where to take you. You are not frightened because this is pretend. Look down. What can you see? (The children can speak out here.) You arrive at the place. The magic carpet sets you down gently. You look round. What do you see? (The children can speak out here.) Now imagine something nice happens. (Pause) What happened? (The children can share their happening.) Now you get back on the magic carpet. It rises. It takes you safely back.

Additional points

As with many stories, we can read this story either as magic (Sophie did go on a magic carpet) or as make-believe (Sophie used her imagination to go on a magic carpet).

Seeing the Sea

Sophie was in the new caravan with Mummy and Daddy. She wanted to go to the seaside but it rained and rained.

"It's too wet to go in this," said Mummy. "We'll all get soaked."

Sophie played with Daddy's pack of magic cards. She got bored but to her surprise, the Jack of Hearts winked at her. The next moment she was flying with him on his magic carpet. It was sunny! She looked down and saw the bright blue sea. There was a little red boat and children playing on the beach. The wind streamed through Sophie's hair. She felt great.

Soon Sophie found herself back in the caravan, and Jack was back in his card.

That night, at bedtime, Mummy said, "We'll go to the seaside, Sophie, as soon as the rain stops. I promise. I know you were disappointed today." Sophie smiled.

"Don't worry. I went with Jack of Hearts in a dream, Mummy. And I'd like to go again with you."

2 THE ADVANCED STORY:

Seeing the Sea

Seeing the Sea

It rained and rained. At first Sophie liked the drumming sound on the roof of the caravan but she was longing to see the sea. She had never been to the seaside before.

"When will it stop raining, Mummy? I want to see the sea."

"If it stops raining tomorrow, Sophie, we'll go to the beach," Mummy said.

The next day, as soon as Sophie woke up, she heard the drumming of the rain again.

"Oh no," she thought. "It's still raining."

"It might stop this afternoon," said Mummy.

But it didn't. Sophie had never seen such heavy rain, like a giant tap had been turned on in the sky.

"We can't go to the beach in this," said Daddy.

Sophie felt cross.

"I'm bored," she sulked.

"You can play with my magic cards," said Daddy. "You like those."

Sophie did like Daddy's magic cards. She liked the three of diamonds which had one diamond missing, but her favourite was the Jack of Hearts. Jack had spikey red hair. He and his black dog sat on a red and black swirly rug with fringes at each end.

As Sophie looked at Jack he closed an eye and opened it again in a wink. Sophie stared in amazement.

"Come on," Jack said, and Sophie found herself floating on Jack's flying carpet. They were floating outside, but there was no rain. It was a warm, sunny day.

"This is my dog," Jack said. "She's called Sophie too."

Sophie the dog wagged her tail and Sophie smiled.

"We can take you to the beach and back on my magic carpet," said Jack. "In no time at all."

Sophie looked down and saw moving cars that looked as small as toys. The houses were tiny too, like dolls' houses. Her heart gave a jump of excitement. She could see the bright blue sea. It was spread out as far as forever.

"The sea, the sea," she shouted, pointing.

Jack smiled his curvy smile and Sophie the dog wagged her tail.

Sophie could see a boat on the sea and children playing on the sand. She loved the curving waves lapping onto the beach.

The wind streamed through Sophie's hair as Jack turned the carpet back towards the caravan. In no time at all she was inside again, holding the card with Jack and his dog.

"Thank you, Jack," Sophie whispered. "That was great."

Once more Jack winked and then he was statue still.

That night when Mummy tucked Sophie in bed she said, "I'm sorry we couldn't go to the beach Sophie. We will come back in the summer, I promise."

"Never mind, Mummy," Sophie said. "I went with Jack of Hearts on his flying carpet. In no time at all. You didn't even have time to miss me."

"What a vivid imagination you have," said Mummy, smiling. Sophie drifted off to sleep. She was smiling too.

3 ## TALKING ABOUT THE STORY

The teacher and children talk about the story:

- Why couldn't Sophie go to the beach?
- How did she go after all?
- What did she see?
- Have you ever been to the seaside?
- What (else) did you see?

Associated stories, songs, poems and nursery rhymes

Stories

The Garden in *Animal Story Book* by Anita Hevett (Young Puffin)
Toby Spelldragon and the Magician (in the Puddle Lane series by Sheila McCullagh) (Ladybird Books)
Bringing the Rain to Kapiti Plain by Verna Aardema (Macmillan)
The Snowman by Raymond Briggs (Ladybird Books)

Songs

Raindrops (in *Child Education* magazine, Infant Project 51) (Scholastic)
Spring (in *Every Colour Under the Sun*) (Ward Lock Educational)
The Sun that Shines across the Sea (in *Someone's Singing Lord* by Beatrice Harrop) (A&C Black)

Poems and nursery rhymes

A Sea in the House by Stanley Cook (in *A Very First Poetry Book* edited by John Foster) (OUP)
A Corner of Magic by Tony Bradman (in *Smile Please!*) (Puffin Books)
Jack Frost by Tony Bradman (in *Smile Please!*) (Puffin Books)
There are lots of nursery rhymes with a **Jack**:

Jack and Jill

Jack and Jill went up the hill
To fetch a pail of water
Jack fell down and broke his crown
And Jill came tumbling after.

Little Jack Horner

Little Jack Horner
Sat in a corner
Eating his pudding and pie
He dipped in his thumb
And pulled out a plum
And said, "What a good boy am I."

The Queen of Hearts

The Queen of Hearts
She made some tarts
All on a summer's day
The Knave of Hearts
He stole the tarts
And took them clean away
The King of Hearts
Called for the tarts
And beat the knave full sore
The Knave of Hearts
Brought back the tarts
And vowed he'd steal no more.

(The Jack of Hearts is sometimes called the Knave of Hearts.)

The Weather

Whether the weather be fine
Or whether the weather be not,
Whether the weather be cold,
Or whether the weather be hot
We'll weather the weather
Whatever the weather
Whether we like it or not.

Incy Wincy Spider has the rain theme (Chapter 2). Other rain rhymes are provided in Chapter 4.

Note: You can find other examples of stories, songs, poems which link to the story or theme – i.e. they could be about the sea, the seaside, magic, holidays, the imagination.

LEARNING GAMES AND ACTIVITIES

Domain 1: Personal, social and emotional development

1   Circle Time games/questions

- Go round the circle and ask the children about their favourite real place.
- Go round the circle and ask the children to "make up" – pretend/imagine – something they do there.
- Go round the circle and ask the children to *make up* a place. What is it like? Who will you take with you to see it?

2   Circle Time talk

Do you ever feel bored? What could you do about it?

Domain 2: Communication, language and literacy

1   Family talk

Ask the children to bring in pictures of their family. Ask them to identify each one. Encourage them to talk about each one.

Ask the children to pretend they know Sophie's family and to **make up** answers to these questions.

- What is Sophie's mummy's favourite colour?
- What is Sophie's daddy's favourite food?
- What does her grandpa watch on the television?
- What game does her grandma play with Sophie?

2   Rain talk

Say the rhyme:

> *Rain, rain, go away*
> *Come back another day.*
> *Our Sophie wants to play*
> *So rain, rain, go away.*

Where else did Sophie want to go? Encourage outside suggestions. (Shopping. Playground. Walk to Grandma's, etc.)

How can we keep dry in the rain? (Rain hat. Umbrella. Shelter.)

Domain 3: Mathematical development

Making playing cards

Give each child four blank pieces of card. First they make "one of hearts" with just one heart. They make two of hearts. They make three of hearts.

(For very young children prepare the cards first and let the children simply colour in the red hearts, or give heart stickers for them to make their own cards.)

Finally, allow the children to draw their own Jack of Hearts on the fourth card.

Domain 4: Knowledge and understanding of the world

1   Weather

Sophie went to the caravan and it wasn't summertime. It was raining. In England it rains in Winter, Autumn, Spring and Summer. We need rain to make things grow. Why else do we need water? (You can revisit material in Chapter 4.) Mention April showers (and snow/ice sometimes in Winter and sunshine/warmth in summer).

2   Seasons

You can develop a project on the Seasons, helping the children to find out more about Winter, Spring, Summer, Autumn and about the weather. Talk about the months of the year and divide these into the four seasons.

3   A calendar

Finally, to reinforce this in an enjoyable way, allow the children to make a calendar. Photocopy page 105 for each child. They paste this onto a rectangle of A4 card. Alternatively photocopy or print onto card. Using your card collection, the children need to find (or draw) four small pictures to represent:

- Winter (e.g. snow scene; ice-skaters; snow sled; Father Christmas).
- Spring (e.g. flowers; umbrella; blossom on trees).
- Summer (e.g. seaside; sunshine; summer clothes – sun hats, sunglasses, etc.).
- Autumn (e.g. bonfire; autumn-coloured leaves on the trees and falling from the trees).

The children stick their pictures on the appropriate "square" and add a ribbon or string to hang their calendar with. Older children could print the correct three months in each box under each season: Winter, Spring, Summer, Autumn.

The Seasons

Winter	
Spring	
Summer	
Autumn	

Domain 5: Physical development

Talk about how snowflakes drift down, twirling. Give each child a paper doily. Moving their doily in a gentle downward movement, like a snowflake, the children can do a snowflake dance. Play appropriate music. Allow them to practise several times. The aim is for them to become more skilful at co-ordinating (graceful) movement of their doily, their own dance with twirls, without bumping into the other dancers!

At the end of the dancing the children could stick the doilies onto poster-sized dark grey paper – some standing individually and some overlapping – to make a snowflake picture. (Alternatively, along a narrower, long grey sheet they could make a snowflake frieze.)

Domain 6: Creative development

1   Pretend play

In small groups (e.g. four children) let the children play some make-believe games. (They could dress up from the dressing-up box.) For example, they are friends going on a trip to the seaside. They can decide who they are and what happens during the whole of the trip – travelling there, playing there, eating there, coming home.

Watch the children as they play. Notice the "imaginative" suggestions they make. ("Now I bash down your sand-pie and you cry." "I'm the mummy and I make the dinner.")

After the playtime, comment to them how good they were at pretending ... "Jim had a good idea when he said, "I'll go in this shop and buy an umbrella."

2   Decorating a sand-pie

If you have a sand corner let the children take turns (e.g. a few each day for a week) to make a sand pie and decorate it with stones, beads, flags, etc.).

Co-operative poster activity

Seaside picture

Mix some sticky blue and some sticky yellow paint. Draw a wavy line across the middle of the poster page. Let the children use pieces of sponge to print the blue sea (above the wavy line) and the yellow sand (below the wavy line).

Cut pictures from magazines of people in swimming costumes, fish, boats, shells, sandcastles, picnics. (Older pre-school children could find and cut out the pictures for themselves.) Help the children to stick swimmers and fish in the sea; boats near the top of the page; and shells and people and dogs on the sand.

Related titles from Routledge

Stories for Circle Time and Assembly: Developing literacy skills and classroom values

Mal Leicester

'It is a pleasure to find a book on morals, values and literacy which works as well as this one ... There is no counter-productive over-simplification, hectoring, preaching or moralizing. Rather, children and teachers are invited to engage with issues.'

Professor Morwenna Griffiths, Nottingham Trent University

Circle time creates a special time in the school week, when children can use a safe environment in which to think about their relationships and their behaviour and be honest about their problems and feelings.

This book provides a range of lively and engrossing stories for use in circle time activities, which are specially written to encourage the cognitive and emotional development of young children.

The author cleverly links key value-based themes in the circle time stories which will stimulate discussion and enhance pupils' literacy skills and citizenship education. The stories in this book will:

- Promote pupils' self confidence
- Develop their interpersonal skills
- Encourage active and responsible participation
- Support deeper reflection
- Enhance their literacy hour activities.

As well as circle time activity, this indispensable book also offers poems and suggested songs that can be used as the basis for a school assembly. Over-stretched KS1 and 2 teachers will find the stories and learning activities time-saving in their clarity and highly enjoyable to deliver.

Pb: 0-415-35535-4
Available at all good bookshops
For ordering and further information please visit:
www.routledge.com